LOOK!

this is the way it is

A PERSPECTIVE OF LIFE THROUGH THE LENSES OF A VERY REAL CHICK

#mentalhealth #falseperceptions #firstGod
#breakingstigmas

AILEEN AMADOR MEZZA

ISBN 978-1-0980-1979-2 (paperback)
ISBN 978-1-0980-1981-5 (hardcover)
ISBN 978-1-0980-1980-8 (digital)

Christian Faith Publishing, Inc.
832 Park Avenue
Meadville, PA 16335
www.christianfaithpublishing.com

Printed in the United States of America

ENDORSEMENTS

"It is a portrayal of Aileen's vulnerability, courage, perseverance, audacity, and strength to turn tragedy into triumph, despair into determination, and craziness into creativity. It is a story worth reading."

—Vance B. Becker Ph. D, Seattle, Washington

"…there is hope and help for people whose stories are like Aileen's."

—Lorenzo Smith; Lead Pastor
Collective Church, Culver City, California

"…all young women should become everything she is capable of while living lives of love, faith, and courage. Aileen is the epitome of that philosophy and so much more."

—T. Mendoza PhD; Principal of Saint Joseph High
(all girl high school), Lakewood, California

"Aileen has exposed her soul in this book. Maybe you can become real with yourself by reading just how Aileen became real with herself."

—Patrick J Silva; Attorney at Law, Redlands, California

"Aileen takes the reader on a dark, twisted, and sometimes hilarious journey into the world of mental illness and learning information for those in need."

—Nicholas Fittante MA, MFT, DCHT
Marriage and Family Therapist, Ontario, California

"Reading this book is akin to having a raw and real conversation with the author that speaks from her heart and soul, uncensored."

—Teresa Arciero MS, LMFT
Marriage and Family Therapist, Menifee, California

"Her authentic story supported by scientific knowledge tells a story about mental health and the stigma that is attached to it is raw, real, and unapologetic, and most importantly courageous."

— Judy Davidds-Wright
The Wright Consulting Group, Anaheim Hills, CA

"I'll be recommending this absorbing memoir for years to come."

—Dr. Yasmin Davidds
CEO of Dr. Yasmin Davidds Leadership
Institute, Los Angeles, California

"It is a rare piece of work that has the possibility of uniting us all together to learn, grow, fight stigma, and overcome the difficulties in the mental health field."

—Jenifer Gayou MPsy, Mental Health Advocate, Boise, Idaho

"This can happen to anyone and DO NOT be afraid to seek help."

—Helga Campbell, Family Relative, Queens, New York

"…I feel any person that is fighting for something right now, must read this book."

—Bobby Blair; Author of Hiding Inside the Baseline
CEO of LQBTQ Loyalty Holdings Inc.
Former world-ranked professional tennis player
Fort Lauderdale, Florida

"… it grabs you from the very beginning and takes you through her life journey."

—Juan M Velez MD, Providence Health Care
St.Joseph's Medical Center, Orange, California.

EDITOR'S NOTE

Dear Readers,

We are excited to introduce LOOK! This is the way it is, a work that has been diligently and passionately crafted by its author. In my role as the editor entrusted with the privilege of bringing this book to fruition, I would like to share some thoughts on the journey that has led us to this significant moment, with a special emphasis on the book's exploration of mental health awareness.

Right from the inception, Aileen embarked on a literary voyage, intricately weaving her experiences and thoughts into a tapestry of vulnerability. As the editor, I've been honored to offer guidance, support, and constructive feedback throughout the creative process. My cousin, Holla Watson, brought the cover of this book to life with mere conversations. Witnessing the transformation of this manuscript, from its initial concept to the refined realness you hold in your hands, has been an incredibly gratifying experience.

Aileen has poured her heart and soul into these pages, addressing themes and subjects that hold both timeless relevance and contemporary significance. Her commitment to authentic storytelling and her ability to navigate the delicate realm of mental health with empathy shine brightly in every chapter. We hope to engage readers and encourage reflection on the critical importance of mental health awareness in all areas of life. We hope to break the stigma that haunts mental health advocacy like a raincloud. We strive to encourage and impact the mental health of individuals and society at large.

My foremost aim has been to preserve the author's unique voice while ensuring clarity, coherence, and consistency. The true measure of any book's success is found in the hearts and minds of its readers. We hope that LOOK! This is the way it is, will resonate with you, challenge your perspectives on mental health, and inspire conversations and actions that contribute to a more compassionate and understanding world. We encourage you to immerse yourself in its pages and allow Aileen's words to take you on a journey of introspection, empathy, and radical self-love.

Thank you for joining us on this literary adventure, one that not only entertains and enlightens but also raises awareness of the critical importance of mental health. Your readership is valued, and we eagerly anticipate your insights and feedback as you explore the pages of LOOK! This is the way it is.

With love and light,
Jenessa Mercer
Editor, LOOK! This is the way it is.

AUTHOR LOVE LETTER

Dear Reader,

This serves as a love letter addressed to you, the individual who made the choice to pick up this book and embark on its contents. I would like to commence by expressing that life often unfolds differently from our expectations. Things may not always align with your well-laid plans, but through diligence and taking courageous, incremental steps, you can overcome any challenges that cross your path. This book serves as more of a public diary, a medium through which I share my life experiences and how I navigated through them. My aspiration is that you discover something valuable to carry with you through your own life journey, whether it serves as a helpful tool in your personal narrative or equips you to support and guide someone you hold dear through their trials and tribulations.

Within these pages, you won't encounter meticulously crafted sentences. Instead, you will encounter the unfiltered and authentic obstacles I have faced and the guiding forces that shaped me into the woman I am today. I am far from perfect, as is every individual. This imperfection is one of the reasons behind the creation of this book. In a world that can often feel cold and judgmental, my desire is for others to realize that they are not alone. I hold profound affection for every phase I have passed through in my life, and I hope you derive pleasure from gaining insight into my experiences as a genuinely authentic woman.

With love and deep gratitude,

Aileen Amador Mezza

DEDICATION

To this crazy world we all get to call home for now and to K.I.D. (Karina Irma Davids), my gorgeous friend that left this crazy world way too soon and now resides at our eternal home. Until we meet again. San Diego, baby!

CONTENTS

FOREWORD

A wise man once said, "It is only when you are truly lost that you find your way."

Aileen Amador's story starts 21 years ago, when she went walking naked and psychotic after a college party, only to find herself a few days later, locked up in a psychiatric hospital. While in the hospital, she begins to hallucinate. She sees demons, Jesus and other visions— all of which trigger her to begin to question her deep Christian faith.

In Look! this is the way it is, Aileen shares her story of what happened when a profound instance of mental illness took over her life, changing her course forever. For Aileen, mental illness is not only a complicated medical condition, it's also a cause for a spiritual crisis. As she struggles to heal, she also seeks a way to understand the cause of her affliction, some of which lead her to question the emotional and mental constraints of her religious upbringing. She meets resistance from her family, friends, and members of her church, who hear Aileen's questions as offensive gestures against religious doctrine. Ultimately, the truth wins out and in it Aileen finds true healing, discovering that in spite of the societal stigma, Christianity and psychiatry can coexist and enhance healing.

Aileen's story inspires those of us who believe in Jesus and struggle with mental illness in ourselves or our loved ones. Her story is one of confusion, courage, faith and ultimately happiness. As her doctor of twenty years it has been my blessing to witness her salvation.

Dr. Michael Lardon, MD.

CHAPTER 1

Perception

Ask, and it will be given to you; seek, and you will find; knock,
and it will be opened to you. For everyone who asks receives, and
he who seeks finds, and to him who knocks it will be opened.

—Matthew 7:7–8 (NKJV)

Sitting on my balcony writing and living the life I've always
dreamed of. *Not!* LOL. If only, right?

I only say that because I suppose that we always figure that as
long as we take the *right* steps early on in life, we will be destined for
a life that is utterly blissful in every sense of the word.

Again, *not!* The absurd thing is that, on occasion, I meet so
many people that paint that pretty peachy keen picture of the perfect
life.

Perfect life?

Is there such a thing?

I thought if I tried really hard, I could be *perfect*.

Again, *not!*

It's crazy because I remember a time that I was teased by my
girlfriends as they jokingly referred to me as a *perfect girl,* for example, perfect girl who has the perfect shoes, perfect car, perfect clothes,
etc." Yet that statement couldn't be more false. Why? Because as long
as I can remember, I have always had a constant struggle with my
weight, so I have always felt that my outer appearance was far from

perfect. Still perhaps, people saw me as this super all-together chick. Again, *not!*

Or maybe they didn't.

Maybe it's that at the time, I perceived that they saw me as this perfect chick. Hence, if I am perceiving it, then it ultimately becomes what *my reality* is. Thus, *perception becomes an individual's reality.*

Here are my thoughts on the above statement. You see, whether a person's perception is true or false is insignificant. Why? Because in the very moment someone is perceiving whatever it be about you, that is it.

It becomes what they ultimately see, for instance, first impressions. Do you base your opinion of people on your first impression of them? I believe it's human nature to do so. Think of the times you met people that were initially unpleasant and later on they just grew on you? I have experienced that many times.

So what does that say about false perceptions? The fact of the matter is that regardless if they're true or false, it's trivial. We can therefore conclude that perceptions, for the most part, are more times than not more false than true.

Perceptions are constantly changing. It is the most puzzling thing to me. I remember as a little girl I was quite the gazer. My eyes were always on everyone and everything. Today I often see that same gaze in my little girl's eyes. My *big-eyed mamasota's* eyes are the very ones on this book cover. You see, as a little girl, I was very intuitive, and I guess that could be perceived as nosy. My nose always wanted to be up in everything. Everyone that knows me can definitely vouch for that.

My daughter does the same. She is five years old, and I am so scared of what she is perceiving at times. Why? Because I can't get into her little brain and make sure all that she is perceiving is right. I just pray her early perceptions are positive ones because now that I am forty, I can honestly admit that my early perceptions of life truly had to have been false ones.

I thought I could live the perfect life because on the outside looking in, life looked so beautiful and easy. As a child, you can't wait to grow up; And then as an adult, you're like, "Whoa! Time sure is going pretty fast. Can we stop it?" especially as a parent, watching your littles grow.

I've always wanted to be perfect and maybe, in my own obscure way, I believed that I was very close to obtaining it. I only say this because my parents somewhat raised me to believe this. It was as it seemed they had as well a false perception of themselves that they were somewhat above others and in another class. This is quite sad to say, but it's the truth. And I am the product of that. I grew up, to a degree, believing the same thing that I was thus a little more perfect than others.

Is that not insane thinking though? Perhaps.

Over the years as I have matured and observed more people around me, I have come to realize that it's not that unusual. People always want to believe that they are better than others.

But why?

Do you really think you're able to achieve utter perfection? You see, in my book, my beliefs are centered on the only man that actually walked this earth and achieved actual perfection in every sense of the word. Yeap, that was Jesus Christ!

Oh my!

Yes, I said it! You're probably thinking, "Oh no! Am I reading a book by some author that is a Holy Roller?" Hmm. Holy Roller, you say? Yeah, I choose to roll with Jesus, but I am far from being a Holy Roller. It may be obvious given this introduction, and that is that I opened this chapter with a biblical scripture.

Ever since I was a young girl, I dreamed up my life and what I wanted it to be. I was raised Catholic, so I was very aware of a higher being to whom I prayed to. Today, that higher being is still the one I pray to. Although while I was growing up, I thought the story of a man whom actually walked this earth, was a healer, a miracle worker, spreader of good news, etc., then was persecuted, crucified, died, buried, and then rose again was somewhat of a fairy tale. Even though as skeptical as I was, I still leaned on Jesus Christ; He has been and will always be my rock.

He is the one I've chosen to rest and put my faith in. I know that as a little girl when I felt alone and cried, I always felt that there was someone there that heard and saw me crying. He is the one that has always known my heart and everything I was and would become.

Nothing in life is coincidence, and I finally get it now.

There are so many cliché statements that people try to share with you while they journey along with you in this life. However, in that moment, they never usually make sense.

My favorite cliché statement? "Everything happens for a reason. You just may not know it now, but it does." Whenever someone would share these words with me, living in that particular moment, I would always feel like responding, "Umm, I don't know, but my life seems pretty messed up right now."

Although I'd like to always believe this particular cliché statement, it's truly hard to believe it when you're all caught up in your mess and are unable to make sense of the whys.

Today, I realize that every human goes through this. I suppose what I'm trying to say is that I know that my heart has always longed and asked for doors to be opened for me if God willed it in my life. And one thing I am particularly certain of is that the desires I have had on my heart since childhood were placed there for a reason. Although I did ask God to lead me to the places where I was destined, at the time, I had never realized that a lot was required of me.

Let us start from the beginning and perhaps shed some light; *I grew up quite spoiled.*

My parents are 100 percent Colombian. That's Colombia in South America and is spelled C-o-l-o-m-b-i-a, not C-o-l-u-m-b-i-a. I have to make that point because the incorrect spelling is every Colombian's pet peeve.

My parents came here in the 1960s. They made a better life for themselves, a life better than they could have ever made back home in Colombia. My father served in the US Army, and when he was no longer on active duty, he married my mother. My parents were the definition of upper-middle-class Latinos living in California. They were able to send my sister and I to twelve years of Catholic school and held good positions at companies like General Motors and Boeing.

However, the main thing I remember as a child was that I was able to get what I wanted whenever I wanted. Most would call me manipulative or spoiled. But how about we just call it me being me and the way I was wired?

No one could have actually taught me to be the very being I was meant to be. It was always in my DNA to be this happy-go-lucky chick that saw life as some kind of amusement park; I lived for the thrill and perhaps still do.

I never knew my limits and was super carefree. I have always been passionate about *everything* that I truly longed for. Sometimes that would get me into trouble, but for the most part, it is my driving force to push me forward, molding me into the overachiever I have always been.

My parents were the typical Latino controlling type plus infinity plus infinity and plus infinity plus infinity plus infinity.

Oh, did I mention that they were over the top strict? Or just infinitely controlling?

In retrospect, I believe I was always pleading to God to open a door for me so that I could bust out of that infinite controlling situation of living under my parents' roof. I never knew what that door would be; and just because I asked and received, didn't mean that I always made the wisest choices when God opened that wide door.

My first open door came to me at the age of seventeen and a half. I graduated high school in 1996 from St. Joseph's High in Lakewood, California, an all-girl Catholic school. I had my plan in place after graduation.

I was ready for college!

I was accepted to the only two universities I applied for—Cal State Fullerton and San Diego State University. I didn't even bother applying anywhere else because I was so certain I would get accepted into those two schools and didn't want to bother to write an essay to get into a UC or private university.

#Truestory.

I hated writing in school. Probably because I write however I want and am grammatically incorrect almost 100 percent of the time.

Go figure. Have you observed my writing style as of yet?

I don't care to pay attention to correct punctuation, so I hated writing and being graded on it. Today, notably, I am able to write for pleasure and pour my whole heart and soul out. I do it even if my thoughts are scattered and all over the place, which are nearly 100 percent of the time as well, all it takes is for me to have a good editor to dissect my writing/thoughts and make them appear more appropriate. Shout out to my editor, Ms. Jenessa Mercer, for going over all my copy edits and helping me organize my first authored book, my masterpiece, I hope. As you read along, you all will be the judge of it. Some may love it, and some may not; it doesn't really matter to me. I am not here to people please. I'm done trying to do that.

Note, you will die trying to, so please stop trying already. You will never be happy chasing the wind.

Ref. "Am I now trying to win the approval of human beings, or of God? Or am I trying to please people? If I were still trying to please people, I would not be a servant of Christ" (Galatians 1:10, NIV).

Why did I take it upon myself to embark on this task and write a book about my journey and battle with mental health?

No. 1, I wrote this book for me, for much internal and personal healing that was of the highest priority in my life at this present moment as I am getting ready to celebrate a milestone birthday on October 27, 2018, turning the *big* 4-0!

No. 2, it is in the hopes of breaking mental-health stigmas so that awareness about being treated is no longer taboo to be spoken about or considered *crazy* to seek help because then it's admitting to your *crazy*. Well, let me tell you all something. Whether it's you, a family member, friend, etc., the most *crazy* thing is keeping it in the dark out of shame. Please go get the help you need, whether it be praying, seeking natural methods, or even medical intervention. Whatever it may be, go get the help before it goes untreated. We are very well aware today in our age what untreated mental illness looks like.

An example is Nicholas Cruz, a mentally ill kid his whole life, unproperly treated, but it's too late now. He lost his marbles, killed innocent high-school kids and school faculty. No, it wasn't the gun itself. It was a fallen human heart and his unbalanced mind. Or another untreated result of mental illness is suicide, which is also too late to treat by then.

Let's face it. This world is a crazy place, and everyone is a little crazy. You just need to learn to balance your own little dose of crazy in a healthy matter. There is hope. I am living proof, and there is *no shame in my game*. Read along; my life has always been an open book.

Look! This Is the Way It Is is my book, my life journey up until this point being told *raw*, a conversation I am having with this crazy world. Yes, the same one that you live in as well.

A large survey of randomly selected adults, sponsored by the National Institute of Mental Health (NIMH) and conducted between 2001 and 2003, found that an astonishing 46 percent met criteria established by the American Psychiatric Association (APA) for having had at least one mental illness within four broad categories at some time in their lives. The categories were "anxiety disorders," including, among other subcategories, phobias and post-traumatic stress disorder (PTSD); "mood disorders," including major depression and bipolar disorders; "impulse-control disorders," including various behavioral problems and attention-deficit/hyperactivity disorder (ADHD); and "substance use disorders," including alcohol and drug abuse. Most met criteria for more than one diagnosis. Of a subgroup affected within the previous year, a third were under treatment—up from a fifth in a similar survey ten years earlier. (Marcia Angell, "The Epidemic of Mental Illness: Why?" *The New York Review of Books,* June 23, 2011, http://www.nybooks.com/articles/2011/06/23/ epidemic-mental-illness-why/)

So 46 percent of the population. Hmm, that is half of humanity. So the other half never got tested, or we're all mentally ill. LOL.

Okay, okay, let's get this show on the road. Or I mean this book, story, whatever. On your mark, get set, go Aileen! Go Aileen!

I digress again. So what happened when I asked and God finally opened that first wide open door?

CHAPTER 2

The Open Door

In the fall of 1996, I landed as a freshman at San Diego State at the age of seventeen going on eighteen. I remember it like it was yesterday, being dropped off by my parents and moving into my college dorm. Once they took off, I remember this overwhelming feeling coming upon me as I lay on my college dorm bed for the first time, and I realized that I finally was *free*!

I had broken free from my crazy Colombian upbringing filled with countless memories of house parties that my parents hosted week after week.

Really, it's all I knew.

We, Colombians, are party people!

My parents knew how to cater and throw a good party too. I grew up in a mix of overly prideful and super dramatic individuals. Hence, that is all I knew.

So guess what? That girl that arrived at the age of seventeen and a half at San Diego State University was just that—a self-absorbed Colombian prideful and dramatic girl. I mean, I didn't know any better at the time.

Perhaps I could have, but I didn't.

Albert Einstein wrote, "Everybody is a genius. But if you judge a fish by its ability to climb a tree, it will live its whole life believing that it is stupid."

With my outward personality being that of an overly extroverted chick came much judgment. But what could I expect? I came from a Colombian bubble full of immense chaos. At that time, the only thing I knew I could accomplish with certainty was that if I maintained good grades, I would get rewarded. I always used it to my advantage.

Can that be considered being manipulative or spoiled?

What exactly does it mean to be either?

Was I *manipulative*? I mentioned that I knew that if I maintained good grades, I would get rewarded. How did I know that though? Simple, kids are smart. Haven't you noticed? I have.

They pick up on everything. I had studied my mom and dad for as long as I can remember. I knew that if I kept my grades up, they really didn't have room to complain. I was doing as they wanted, wasn't I?

I was rewarded because my grades were always above average. I wasn't the straight-A kid but definitely a pretty consistent A and B student except for my grade in conduct. LOL.

My father, for the most part, was always the main stickler for grades. In Colombia, my dad was the A+ or A+++ student of his class. I say that because I even remember him saying that he had close to a 5.00 gpa. How that is possible? Don't ask me.

Although I was always a consistent A and B student, I remember a year in elementary school that my conduct grade came as a C, but all the rest were As and Bs. This memory is vivid in my brain.

My dad looked at my report card and said in Spanish, "Well, it's okay. The C is in conduct. It doesn't really matter. At least you're smart and getting good grades in all your other classes."

Parents! Warning! If you have a straight-A student or A-and-B student but your kid's conduct grade is C or even B-, please red flag that. No, seriously! I think my dad thought it was all right because it was really just my personality.

What I am trying to get at is that he didn't care that my conduct was faulty. He just cared that I was getting good grades in all the other subjects.

But was I really smart? Manipulative? Or just a *spoiled* brat?

If you ask me, I was all of these things. If you were to ask an outsider looking in, they may perceive that I was only *spoiled*. I say this because it's what stood out. I knew how to get my way; hence, I was manipulative first, then that led me to be spoiled.

Do you follow?

Or have I lost some of you?

You might be this person or may have a kid just like that. Although, I pray really hard you don't. LOL.

You see, No. 1, I was smart. No. 2, because I was smart, I knew how to be manipulative, and No. 3, being smart and manipulative resulted in me being spoiled.

That is a formula for disaster! Like the saying goes, "I was too smart for my own good." I'm not saying all these things to toot my horn either. This is real stuff. For reals, I was and I am still this person. These three characteristics led me to a very catastrophic life for many years.

Why?

Because this was my pattern for a very long time. Do you know the true definition of insanity? "Doing the same thing over and over again but expecting different results." I was downright *crazy*, but everyone thought I was just so fun. I still am fun. The good thing is that today, I know my boundaries and limitations, whereas as a kid, I didn't.

Whatever the case, there are many things I realized early on in life. This one coming up next is a biggie—that everyone talks about everyone, and to some degree, *we're all hypocrites*!

Yes, I am including myself in the previous statement.

I hate being placed in situations that I have to truly pretend to be fine and, for a lack of better words, sometimes even fake. I hate fake people, and I just am not one of them, so I'd rather not act. I hate the action of being fake because it forces hypocrisy.

But we all do it!

And yet, there are some that pretend as if they don't.

Here is another one.

Every woman on this planet gossips.

Yes! That means you Ms., Mrs., Miss, etc.

"Who me? I'm just highly opinionated and just comment."

Yeah, don't sugarcoat your gossip ladies. It's in our innate nature, and I don't believe a woman that says she never gives her opinion about another. I have met women that truly feel they're excluded from actually partaking of actual gossip because they believe they are just plainly conversing with other women and sharing opinions.

Well, guess what?

That's just another way of saying that you're gossiping!

And here it goes from a super duper transparent chick: I gossip, and I cannot deny it.

I don't always mean to, but I do. I share opinions more often than not. Hence, I guess that would have to be considered gossip.

Yep, it sure is; no denial here.

However, it just seems that with me, for some reason, whenever I partake in gossip, I am always framed as the bad guy while other women deny that them sharing their *opinions* with each other is not gossip but rather a casual conversation.

I was hit especially hard with the misperception and gossip of women during my college years right after everything started to fall apart. I'm a loyal friend, always have been, and this was no different during college.

My first semester of college, my girlfriends and I all decided to pledge an already established multicultural sorority (non-Panhellenic). For those who are aware or not aware of the whole college sorority life, we all became *pledge sisters. Pledging* is the term used to define the process a pledge sister must go through to basically be worthy of obtaining the Greek letters that stand for the sorority. Remember, I mentioned that *you must be down and worthy* for the sorority to become a sorority sister. Within our pledge class, there was one of our pledge sisters that at that time, according to the *big sisters* of the sorority, was not exemplifying being down and worthy of the letters. The result of that is that this pledge sister of ours ended up getting dropped from the class and was not worthy of continuing with the pledging process for that class. As I type this, I realize that I may be mocking the situation. But really, I am not. It's just that at eighteen years old, I saw it as the coolest thing. Today, twenty years later, umm, not so much.

So in lieu of them dropping our pledge sister, I called a meeting for us all to agree to drop the already established sorority as well. And for over a year, my friends and I were labeled as crazy party girls partying with all the fraternity guys.

It sounds so silly to even reminisce on this now. However, I can't prove my next point if I don't take you all down memory lane with me. A whole year went by. It was now the fall of 1997, my sophomore year. It then dawned on me throughout the previous whole year, "Why did we need to belong to any sorority?" If we wanted to, I thought to myself at the time, we were all cool enough girls to do our own thing.

I rolled with a pretty tight-knit group of girlfriends. The entire pledge class didn't remain close, but there was about a good eleven of us girls that remained good friends. I then began to propose to my besties at the time the idea that we should found our own sorority at San Diego State. It was during that season that I had been approached by another already established sorority from a Northern California university that wanted to start their very first chapter at San Diego State University.

I then began talking regularly to the founding mothers of the sorority up north interested in meeting a group of girls again *down* and *worthy* to establish the founding chapter of their sorority at San Diego State University. After months of speaking with them, they were convinced that they needed to come visit to meet my friends and I.

At this point of my life, I was on a super high from it all. I thrive on being a determined individual that makes things happen. Also, I think the big fact was that I actually was the initiator, and it felt really good. You know that feeling, right? It's like I was accomplishing something even though my grades were suffering because all my smarts went out the door during those years. In retrospect today, I realize that I gave it so much more importance perhaps than some of my other friends.

Inevitably though, things don't always happen as planned. It was on January 13, 1998, that I experienced the most horrific incident of my life. One that I let define myself for so many years because of the trauma and aftermath that comes from being the girl that tripped out hard on shrooms (psilocybin mushrooms) and being taken in 5150.

This all happened days before my friends and I were scheduled to go up to Northern California to finalize everything with the sorority. I was admitted to a county mental facility in San Diego because I was so stuck on a schroom trip.

The proper term for it was that I was undergoing a drug-induced psychosis, and the doctors were unsure that I would ever come out of it. While I was in a mental hospital fighting a spiritual battle to come back and praying to God to not take my sanity, my so-called besties, rather than wait and postpone the trip, decided to take the drive up there without me.

I was devastated when I finally got a bit better and realized they went without me. How could they? Why without me? Not to boast, but I was at the very core of us all. I, Aileen Amador, was the one initiating it all.

In the end, all the months of my hard work and dedication getting us all to the point of getting interviewed/pinned was ignored. My girlfriends ended up establishing the founding chapter of that sorority on the SDSU campus, and in the end, they took all the credit.

In reality, I didn't get stuck, and as you read along, you will get all the details of what really happened. The questions that ended up running through my head when I found out that they had all made the decision to proceed with the pledging process without me were questions like:

Why did they do it?

Did they try not to do it?

Were they all in agreement?

Was there another alternative?

And if there wasn't another alternative, then why couldn't they have all dropped like we did previously, for our pledge sister, Karina?

Until this day, I am very selective about the woman I let in my life. I have never been one to be part of a clique. I have an array of so many beautiful women in my life, but I prefer one-on-one rela-tionships. If anything, I have so many besties. I mean it, women that I enjoy having one-on-one time with. That means only two people dialoguing.

You know the saying "Three is a crowd" really does have some truth to it. If there is only two women in a dialogue, it's only one perception on another perception. When there is three, you get one extra perception. What does that mean? That that third perception has the ability to influence one of the other two, if not both. Hence, the result being *gossip*, proving my point.

The aftermath of that whole incident is what added to the years of trauma. Right about now, you're probably wondering, "Why does perception matter to her so much?" This is my why...,

I was deemed *crazy* by many; that meant most family, close fam-ily friends, and so-called friends. And slowly, the gossip and every-one's perception of me peeled off the masks that they had been wear-ing for years, and I got to see who was really true to me and who wasn't.

Why is this important? Because it's all about perception. Your perception, my perception, her perception—all that is being shared in casual conversation.

But again, is your perception really my reality? Or is it just yours? At what point do we start to understand that our perceptions are not each other's reality?

CHAPTER 3

5150

I sit here contemplating how far I've come, and I consider myself very blessed.

Very, very, very blessed.

There's truth in the saying that "some things happen for a reason, and in that moment, you don't know why," but they do.

My twentieth-year anniversary of the most traumatic incident that has ever happened to me was on January 13, 2018, something that I hoped for many years to find out why.

Let me take you back to the sequence of events leading up to that incident on January 13, 1998.

It was the fall of 1997. I had just begun my sophomore year at San Diego State. Five of my girlfriends and I became roommates. We rented a nice townhome not too far from campus. Three of my best guy friends also rented the same model townhome on a neighboring street. My guy friends' place was actually a lot cozier to me. I always felt so much more peace at their place than ours.

I loved hanging with my girlfriends. We were all so different in our unique way. We would bump heads a lot for the normal stuff girls bicker and are drama about. But in the end, I believed we all had a genuine love for one another. Due to that reason, I know it is why it stung so bad when they chose to proceed with the sorority without me. I felt so betrayed. The ones that I actually lived with I can say were my *roll dwags,* meaning, we all were very close and hung out a lot together. LOL. But man oh man were we Drama. Yes, with a capital D. Imagine, six girls living together in a four-bedroom townhome. Plus I just don't handle drama very well. And when there is drama around me, there is no escaping in the moment. I get sucked in. I partake by always putting in my two cents. We would get into some nasty bickering and arguments over the dumbest things. I can't deny it either. I was always the more super sensitive one, so I would retaliate all the time. Hence, causing even more drama. I never knew how to be quiet. And I still kind of don't. LOL. But thank God that my three best guy friends were just on the next street. So their home became my daily escape from the drama. Two of the three guy friends were like big-brother figures to me. The third guy friend was a fraternity brother of theirs that I had met freshman year but didn't really get close to until that summer of 1997 when they all moved in together. Richard and Derek were the two I considered like big brothers during that season. Derek was a year older and Richard four years older than me. I would head over to vent to them about everything. I never understood why girls could be so catty and mean. So when my girlfriends became too much, I would just go hang over at Richard and Derek's. Then Sam was the third roommate. Since I spent so much time over visiting with Richard and Derek, naturally Sam and I became very well acquainted.

(Insert) Note to reader: This part was added prior to submitting final draft to publisher. I had been unsure whether to include this in the book, but a good friend mentioned that it was important to share what happened prior to the evening I shroomed and what events/things might had triggered the crazy trip.

So now moving on…

I was saying that Sam and I quickly developed a friendship. It was strictly platonic. However, we did become super close friends rather quickly. For the first time ever, I started to feel that I had like a deep soul connection with someone. I am deep by nature. Hence, I should have probably never experimented with any drugs because I think my brain always was out there daydreaming and tripping already about something. I'm a feeler and put intense emotion into everything I do. I don't know if it was just the part of me being a girl, but I was always that girl that fell pretty hard for the guy. And in this case, falling hard for the guy was an understatement. Sam and I became quite inseparable that first semester of sophomore year. He really became my best friend. From walking on campus together, getting a bite to eat, or just hanging out in his room, talking for hours, night after night. We would literally lay down together night after night just talking until the sun came up. I would end up falling asleep next to him, but we were never intimate physically or sexually. It was the oddest thing. Our friends actually couldn't believe that we weren't hooking up. I think there was a time I denied having any attraction toward him initially. But then as we bonded, something started to grow. I think it was in November of 1997 that one night we actually had our first kiss after months of being strictly platonic friends. But it was a first kiss that, as cheesy as it sounds, left me mesmerized. Partly because my mind had built up this moment. Again, we were kids. I was nineteen years old. He was twenty years old. I always had a tendency to be super deep. But it happened one night as we laid down next to one another just like any other night. The aftermath was a bit odd, I think, for the both of us. We were in that weird place, where you experience hooking up with one of your closest friends but wished you could take it back, because you don't want to ruin the friendship.

But again. How old were we? Like nineteen and twenty. Young and dumb college kids. I vividly remember thinking, "We're cool. We're just friends, like, no biggie," to not make it awkward. But I couldn't fake it for too long. I have to admit Sam became my first unrequited love or one-sided love. Webster defines it as *not reciprocated or returned in kind.* I don't think I really knew what I was feeling. However, I did know it was intense. But I tried to play it cool around Sam after the fact. We went back to being friends and tried to not revisit the incident. He never really reciprocated anything, so naturally, I took it as rejection, which is not easy to take for anyone. Yet I acted like everything was all fine. Sam knew how crazy my girlfriends drove me and never quite understood why I didn't cut them off. But there I was, so pumped about the founding chapter of the sorority we were to establish. He didn't understand why I partied so hard. He actually didn't do anything but maybe drink and occasionally smoke some weed. While here, I was in his room with my little drug-paraphernalia kit I would bring that consisted of razors, straws, and credit cards to smash up the lines of whatever I had that was made available for me to snort. It was mainly crystal meth back then. Sam knew that something wasn't right with me, but what could he do? I think on one occasion, he mentioned about why didn't I just go back home. I was like *hell no*. I left for a reason. In reality, where I was, was not any better. It really all comes down to state of mind. You can escape the places or situations, but in your mind, it's all there. And that was me. I wasn't escaping anything. I was being fooled by the synthetic feeling of the high from the meth, which was not a real escape. We all come down eventually from our high. Then we're faced to deal with our reality. Honestly, that is why most people stay high so they don't have to deal with it in the moment. However, deep down, you are internally dealing with it all. Whether you're conscious of it or not; your body, mind, and soul are.

So now a month went by, and it was winter break. Sam and I were acting like nothing had happened. Yet I got to admit that my feelings were growing stronger and stronger. I was actually glad winter break had come because he was due to go back home for some weeks. Winter break is usually a month. So I remember he was packing to head home for a couple weeks in late December. I was in his room just talking away as always. He knew that I planned on sticking around San Diego throughout winter break and offered his room to stay in while he was gone. He knew that my girlfriends would again tick me off, and I wouldn't be able to handle it and would want to come over. I remember thinking that it was the sweetest thing for him to offer. Yet I was dying inside because although I pretended like I didn't want anything, I really did. So the fact that he never pursued me started to get to me. In my head, I started thinking things like all crazy chicks think when they get sprung or are in love for the first time. I thought things like; we're so perfect for one another. We're best friends. We're soul mates, etc. Why can't he see it? So what I did was act like it didn't bother me. I acted confident around him, and all I talked about was the fact that we were about to become founding mothers and that I planned to change next semester when we begin pledging, that I would quit doing drugs and get my act together.

Now, the magic mushrooms from Sam…

I had done shrooms two times previously, and I had been fine. But the third and last time was different. I was tripping from the get-go, probably even before actually ingesting them. You see, Sam had a friend that had given him some bags of supposedly the best mushrooms from Arizona to sell to us college kids in San Diego. The two previous times I had done them I had good trips, so I wasn't worried about doing them again. I actually was in a super euphoric mood. So the story went like this. I asked Sam the day he was packing his things in his room if he could please give me a free bag of the mushrooms he had. I promised him that I just wanted to do them one last time. He was hesitant. But I am quite persuasive, so I convinced him to give me a bag so I can plan a night of shrooming to go all out with my friends one last time.

So Sam gave me his magic mushrooms. At least in my head, I started to believe that was the truth. So I planned the night and we had a shroom party. We put them in between rice krispie treats. Then we sprinkled them in a bowl over weed and smoked out of a bong. We ingested them with oranges because of the vitamin C which would enhance the trip. Everyone had came over to our townhome where I lived with my girlfriends. We chilled and had our shroom party there. I remember we were watching *Romeo and Juliet*, the movie, the one that starred Leonardo DiCaprio. And I started to trip really hard while watching the movie. I started to get in this trance about the intense feeling toward Sam I was feeling that at the moment wasn't even being reciprocated. Something just snapped, and I kept sharing with others throughout the night that the movie was like Sam and I, like we wanted so much to be, but we couldn't, like something wasn't allowing it. I mean, duh, I wasn't really going to die for his love. LOL. But I was tripping hard and feeling him super hard. So another name for shrooms is magic mushrooms, so I kept saying to everyone that Sam gave me magic with his mushrooms. Naturally, my friends and I thought I would come off of this trip like normal. After a night of shrooming, the trip is usually over the next day. Not for me, I kept tripping for a couple days. But I don't blame my friends. I mean, in hindsight, they could have gone to get me evaluated when two days passed and they saw me sleep deprived and still stuck. But I am sure out of fear, they didn't take me anywhere until the worst thing of all happened. After a night of taking Sam's offer to stay in his room while he was away and I was still tripping on the shrooms, I slept in his room. The next morning, something overcame me to believe that the end of the world was coming and that everyone was running outside naked. And that is exactly what I did. I ran outside naked but covered in a blanket thinking the end of the world was coming. I was stopped by the San Diego PD and taken 5150 (5150 is an involuntary seventy-two-hour hold in a psychiatric facility for evaluation. Three criteria apply to this section: a danger to themselves, a danger to others, or gravely disabled.) to a San Diego County mental health clinic. It was there that my trip had gone so far that I thought I had married Sam. As I was admitted, I even mentioned that my name was Aileen Rodriguez (Sam's last name) and that they needed to call my husband Sam Rodriguez to come get me. Imagine that, Sam was called and told that his wife Aileen was admitted. Can this story get any crazier? Well, it does. Read along.

To conclude this insert, Sam wanted nothing to do with me after that. It took years for us to even get reacquainted. Nothing ever became of us because in the bigger spectrum of things, God had different plans. Today I am married to my true love. And for Sam, I really don't know where he is, but I also pray he found true love. (The end of this impromptu insert.)

Now the following is a real interview between Patrick Silva and Aileen Mezza. Patrick Silva is an attorney that Aileen retained in December of 2017.

Patrick Silva. Hello, this is attorney Patrick Silva. Today I have Aileen Mezza. She is a survivor of 5150 and being traumatized in one of San Diego's worst facilities. Aileen, do you want to talk to us about this today?

Aileen Mezza. Yes, definitely.

Patrick Silva. Tell me when you walked in to the facility, what did it feel like for the very first time?

AILEEN MEZZA. I was taken in 5150. And I wasn't okay because I thought that the end of the world was coming because I had been tripping for days after a night of shrooming with my friends.

PATRICK SILVA. How old were you then?

AILEEN MEZZA. I was nineteen.

PATRICK SILVA. Were you still living at home with your parents, or what were you doing?

AILEEN MEZZA. I was in college, partying it up with my friends at San Diego State.

PATRICK SILVA. It was a good time in your life, wasn't it?

AILEEN MEZZA. Yes, very good time.

PATRICK SILVA. Tell me about mushrooms. How does that make you feel?

AILEEN MEZZA. I had done the mushrooms two times previous, and I loved them. I felt like I was at Disneyland every time I did them. That third time that I ended up taking them, I was taken in by the San Diego PD on Montezuma Road, right down the street from San Diego State.

PATRICK SILVA. Who were you with?

AILEEN MEZZA. Alone. I never came off my trip. I did it with seven of my buddies, two nights prior. They all came off the shrooms.

PATRICK SILVA. For somebody like me, I've never done mushrooms. What's the feeling? How long does it last?

AILEEN MEZZA. Euphoria, super euphoric feeling.

PATRICK SILVA. Like marijuana?

AILEEN MEZZA. Better.

PATRICK SILVA. Like alcohol?

AILEEN MEZZA. Better. You just feel like you're in this umm—

PATRICK SILVA. Is it numbing, or is it like enlightening?

AILEEN MEZZA. Enlightening. For me, it was enlightening. A lot of people that trip on these mushrooms, sometimes it's about seeing stuff and just, "Oh, the trees are tripping, or blah, blah, blah." For me, it was obviously more spiritual and powerful. It always took me to another level of enlightenment. And during that time, a lot was going on. I was getting disqualified from the university. I was stressed, anxious. I thought I was in love. And I believed that, that all created a larger chemical imbalance. Maybe that's why I flipped so hard because I was already imbalanced from all this stuff that was happening. I got taken in, handcuffed and all.

PATRICK SILVA. How did they find you?

AILEEN MEZZA. I was walking down the street covered in a blanket. I was naked, but I was covered. And the San Diego PD stopped me, and I was on my way to my friend's house. They lived on the main street on Montezuma Road. And when I stopped, I said, "Wait here." The cops followed me. I said, "My friends live here. They're going to put clothes on me." My friends put clothes on me. It was a house that we used to party at called *The Barn.* After they all put clothes on me, the cops cuffed me, and they all tried to say, "Oh, she's just been studying." They're all trying to cover up for me, "She's been studying a lot." Cops knew I was under something. They took me into San Diego County mental facility. I'm not sure which one. I think it was over there by old town. And I remember feeling like, when they checked me in, I was in purgatory like I was dying. I felt like, "Where am I?" I felt like, whether I was tripping, I don't know. I was tripping definitely, but I felt like I was in between heaven and hell.

PATRICK SILVA. It sounds like what we see on TV, the white room with the guys walking around.

AILEEN MEZZA. It wasn't padded. I always tell people it wasn't padded. They had me in a waiting room, and then they threw me in a little room with a steel door and four walls and a little cot. Again, it wasn't padded. People always ask like, "Was it padded?" I was not in a white coat either. But they threw me in a room with a steel door and little window. And I yelled at the top of my lungs, "Please don't take my sanity." And I remember looking at the wall. I was raised Catholic, so I knew there was a God, but I really knew there was a God when I saw this light just telling me, "You're going to get out of this." In those mental places, you really see people that are dark. You see people that are very very dark. I think they're whether demon possessed or I don't know, and I knew I wasn't one of them. After the seventy-two-hour hold, I was released. Three of my best friends came to pick me up.

PATRICK SILVA. Let's stop there for half a second. Do you think you had any rights when you went in there?

AILEEN MEZZA. No.

PATRICK SILVA. Did you see anything on the wall that's saying…any signs on the wall that talked about your rights and that while you're there, what rights do you have?

AILEEN MEZZA. At that particular facility, I didn't. It was two years later, I—

PATRICK SILVA. Let's stay on the first incident.

AILEEN MEZZA. So that particular time, no. They had me on a seventy-two-hour hold. I still don't understand. I was nineteen, so they ended up releasing me to my friends, which was really odd. So I don't know why.

PATRICK SILVA. How long were you in there for?

AILEEN MEZZA. It felt like it was only twenty-four hours, or maybe it was the seventy-two hours. I can't even remember. I'd have to check my…honestly, I'd have to go back to my records because I don't even know. I don't even know what happened that first time.

PATRICK SILVA. Did you have a spiritual enlightening? Did you think God…you were in God's presence?

AILEEN MEZZA. Yes. I thought that I was in between heaven and earth. I thought if I was going to stay in that mental hospital, I was dying. I eventually came out but was still not okay. I was from Orange County at the time, so my parents ended up finding out what happened, got transferred over to a facility in Mission Viejo. It was a Charter Behavioral Health. They used to have those back in the day. I got put in a locked facility. And I still wasn't a hundred percent. I just remember being scared. There were crazy people pacing the hallways by my room, and I prayed to God to take me out of this. And I still didn't seem okay. I remember the doctors telling my parents, "I don't know if your daughter's coming back." But I knew I was fighting a spiritual battle, and I knew I was coming back. It's really odd when you're in that state of mind. I was praying to God to bring me back to the light. There is a fine line between light and darkness. And I would see the darkness in people, but I knew I wasn't like them, if that makes any sense. I fought really hard to stay, and I think I brought myself out of it through much spirituality and much prayer. That's why I pray. I'm a Christian now, but I do believe mental illness is not just chemical. It's more than that because I saw demons in people. I saw people that probably will never come out if they don't have a spiritual encounter and fight those demons off. I believe that as the non-Holy Roller that I am, I believe in God, but I don't preach, or I don't think I'm better than anybody. I'm a Christian who believes that there's power in Jesus' name. And I did believe that when I was in that hospital. I would recite, "Lord Jesus, please help me. Lord Jesus." And there are many biblical verse(s) that refer to demons trembling at His name. And I believe I pushed those demons out of me. That's how powerful I believe. I never believed I would be a Christian Holy Roller because I used to think Christians were really over the top. But having that awakening, I knew then and now that the only person that brought me out/back was Jesus Christ, our Lord. It was demonic and heavy. When you open that avenue of doing psychedelics, it's demonic. It's a world that, knock on wood—

PATRICK SILVA. There's a bright side and a dark side when you open that door? Sometimes you see the bright side, and sometimes you see the dark side? You don't know where that is going?

AILEEN MEZZA. Exactly. And mine was a happy trip at first, but then it got distorted. And I went way off, so off that my world was about to end. Because to me, if I would have ended up permanently in a mental asylum, that's like hell here on earth. I would never wish that on my worst enemy. It's like the movies but ten times worse. I can't even watch movies like *A Beautiful Mind* sometimes, because they're too real. And when you live it, it's scary.

Now I do believe that I was imbalanced. I believe I was going through a psychosis. Hence, the doctor that ended up treating me after being released from Charter. (Patrick Silva interjects-)

PATRICK SILVA. Stop right there. So now, your next train of thought when you start speaking is going into how meds helped you.

AILEEN MEZZA. Yes.

PATRICK SILVA. Yeah, stop.

(End of interview)

So… Who is Patrick Silva? He is an attorney that I retained to represent me on a matter. You will learn more about the specifics of who exactly he is soon. So read along.

CHAPTER 4

Signs

I'm in utter disbelief sometimes. I have lived through two decades since that horrific incident, and yet, I remember it like it was yesterday. However, I mentioned before that I felt that I really did let it define me for so many years. Life really has come full circle for me.

I had shared with Dr. Lardon the interview that I did with Patrick Silva, my attorney, where he probed me and asked me questions and got most of the traumatic parts of my story out.

Everything in my life has truly been godsent, and that is why I stand in complete awe today.

Oddly enough, I am grateful to a degree that God chose me for whatever reason to go crazy, to be crazy, to be perceived as crazy and still come out with my chin up.

He's blessed me. I have a beautiful family that I am able to assist in providing for. I no longer feel forced to live up to a title or a credential because that doesn't define me either.

He knew what I would fall into.

He knew what would become of me, and through it all, He saw that I would lean on Him. No matter if I fell, I would go back to Him, and I would persevere in this world.

It's just so crazy to stay on track, and as I do believe in Jesus Christ and I am a Christian, I find myself a lot in the trenches in the sense that there are times that I don't want to walk that fine line.

One thing I know for sure is that if I don't stay on track, there is an adversary that will come and do whatever is possible to try to lure me in.

"Be sober, be vigilant; because your adversary the devil walks about like a roaring lion, seeking whom he may devour." (1 Peter 5:8)

In God only is my strength.

I'm grateful for my husband. He is a great man. Without him next to me, this book would not be possible. You see, my hubby and I are complete opposites, he will always be the first to tell me, "Babe, you're starting to go off the deep end." And guess what? I actually listen because I know he can always pick up on the early signs.

There are days I am so immensely blessed that I just break down, and I start crying tears of joy. I have owned up to it all. And my mental health could not be better in this moment in time.

Throughout the last two decades, I have had to commit to periods of where I needed of course God first always but at times a combination of treatments. My treatment plan has always been a combination of prayer, psychotherapy, and medication in different seasons of my life.

There are currently three pivotal men that have played such a huge role in my life while working towards the goal of obtaining and maintaining my optimum mental health.

No. 1 is Dr. Vance Becker, PhD, who was my first psychologist and like a second father to me. He was the first man to observe my behavior and would tell me in his own way, "Your problem is you don't trust yourself." It's like I felt I couldn't give my thoughts credibility after the drug-induced psychosis aka going crazy. I always wanted to try to change myself and never accepted, understood why I thought the way I did. Dr. Becker would continuously tell me that I just needed to accept I was just plain wired this way.

In early 2017 when I ventured into this journey of writing my book, I had been trying to locate Dr. Becker. He had recently retired. However, I was not having any luck. Then in early 2018, my husband began to google him and found a phone number on his old website that happened to be Dr. Becker's direct cell phone. I had not heard Dr. Becker's voice in over a decade. I literally almost cried when he picked up the phone. I said, "Hello, is this Dr. Becker?"

He said, "Yes."

I said, "This is Aileen Amador. You remember me?"

He said, "Of course, how can I ever forget Aileen Amador?" The story of me getting a hold of him still gives me goose bumps. He met this Aileen at the age of seventeen years old when she thought she knew it all, but really, she knew *nothing*!

God is so awesome.

No. 2 is Dr. Michael Lardon, MD. Words cannot describe the *immense* gratitude, first to God for giving Dr. Lardon the wisdom to treat me in 1998 when no other doctor who had seen me could figure out how to treat me. My parents told him in 1998 that he was an angel sent from God. He said, "No, I am just a doctor." He has been in my life ever since. He is more than just a doctor. He really has been the best life coach I could ever have asked for the last twenty-one plus years of my life. And it is because of him my story has come out into the light. You see, you can't write a story about going crazy without having a psychiatrist backing you up. LOL. But not only is he just mine or any psychiatrist. In over the twenty years I have known him, he now is a sports-medicine psychiatrist who has worked with many well-known PGA, NFL, and Olympic elite athletes.

He wrote the book *Finding Your Zone: Ten Core Lessons for Achieving Peak Performance in Sports and Life*. The zone is defined by Dr. Lardon as *an optimal state of mind in which anyone can achieve their personal best*. He has embedded this statement into my brain over the last twenty years. I jokingly told him once that I'm now his first ordinary mental patient (non-athlete) that he also helped achieve peak performance, not in sports but in life. I have had the best training. Dr. Lardon has written the foreword of this book. And without his 100 percent support, it would have been 100 percent unlikely that I would ever publish my story. He has always believed in me and my potential to speak out to help others.

No. 3 is Nicholas Fittante, MFT. Nick is my current therapist. And although he came into my life maybe only about three-plus years ago, he has helped the Aileen of today find her balance in this madness of a world we live in, especially as a wife, stepmom, mom, and working woman. Nick was placed in my husband and mine's life at the perfect time. The MFT stands for *marriage and family therapist*. Notice the M is first. LOL. My hubby and I sought guidance from a therapist when our marriage seriously needed a tune up. Nick continues to meet with us throughout the year. He has been an immense support to me while on this journey of completing the book.

These three men, the psychologist, the psychiatrist, and the therapist, they're all educated men in the field of psychology.

They have played pivotal roles in different stages of my life, to my well-being, and my mental health, and for them, I'm grateful.

To say that the field of psychology does not offer resources to those willing to seek the help is false. My life is a walking testimony that I did seek #firstGOD, but inevitably God confirmed that the resources the field had to offer were necessary, in my case even submitting to proper western medical treatment. However, my belief is that the individual does need to be willing and pray about God leading them to the proper professionals in the field of psychology to treat them in the season they may find themselves in.

My academic counselor, Carol Davidson, at Hope International University in Fullerton where I currently study human development once shared this quote with me that said, "Sometimes the bad things that happen in our lives put us directly on the path to the best things that will ever happen to us" (Nicole Reed).

So many good things have happened, and I just pray that as my life unfolds that God would give me health, give me wisdom in every area, give good health to my husband and kids, help me provide, organize, and keep my heart on track.

God has confirmed up until this point that everything that has happened has a reason, and it will all be revealed but all in His timing.

CHAPTER 5

My Brain's Not Okay

*T*he *following is another real interview between Patrick Silva and Aileen Mezza.*

PATRICK SILVA. You screamed at the top of your lungs, "Please don't take my sanity." What were you feeling at that exact time?

AILEEN MEZZA. I was in trouble. I was in trouble. Reality hit me when they shut that door. At that point, I just knew. Oh my gosh. I did get on my knees. I even believe I shouted. As I've said in the previous, I think it's so spiritual, mental illness. So I think my soul—

PATRICK SILVA. Who was taking your mental sanity? Was it going to be those guys in white coats, or was it going to be the universe?

AILEEN MEZZA. Demonic, like the universe. Yes.

PATRICK SILVA. The universe was?

AILEEN MEZZA. Yes, the universe, like this demonic presence, darkness. Darkness exist, just as the light, but it was like I was caught in between both. Darkness and light can never coexist. The ruler of darkness is our adversary, the devil, and it is as I felt that I was going to be in hell. I was going to be in my own hell. That's basically what happened throughout my trip. I was tripping for a good I think week or two because then they transferred me to that Charter Behavioral Health. I'm not sure how long I was there. But even there, it was like I was still tripping, and in this

47

trance, I could clearly see people that were in darkness like there was a separation between light and darkness, and I tried really hard, like I shared before in my previous interview, to stay in the light and pray. Like I said, my faith was important because I was raised Catholic, and I knew there was a God. That's how I got myself out. *I'm not staying here.* Like I was crying out, "God, I'm not staying here. This is not where I belong." It was kind of like…oh my gosh help me. I don't—

PATRICK SILVA. Do you think you hit a different—

AILEEN MEZZA. Spiritual realm? Yes.

PATRICK SILVA. Yeah. Transcendence. You were somewhere else then. Right now, here's our reality, you and me talking. When you do drugs like that—

AILEEN MEZZA. Psychedelics, yeah.

PATRICK SILVA. Yeah. They take your mind to a different playing field. That playing field, if you and me are talking here on earth, that playing field might be up in the clouds, or that playing field might be underground. Sounds to me like you went underground on that issue and that trip.

AILEEN MEZZA. Really underground to where I thought I was dying.

PATRICK SILVA. And you thought you were going to stay there?

AILEEN MEZZA. Yes.

PATRICK SILVA. And not come out?

AILEEN MEZZA. Exactly. I was pleading to God to get me out of there, and that's what got me out. I was pleading. I shouted. When I shouted, I was like…oh my gosh, holy moly. *Get me out of here, Lord.* Like get me out. Like I said, I remember looking at the wall. It was a gray wall, and it was there… I saw this light. I saw like what they call one of those apparitions or something like this glow. It was weird. I saw this light saying, "You're going to be okay," even though I wasn't okay for weeks and days after and on the outside looking in. Even the doctors didn't know if I was going to come out of it. I knew I was fighting this spiritual battle within and that my soul wasn't going to die there.

I think that a lot of people that are in mental asylums that's what happens. They let their mind go. Then chemically, they don't get back because they are either still on the drugs, or they don't have the right doctor that really gets them on the right antipsychotic medicine. When I finally, finally, finally got out of the hospital probably at that Charter—I was there for a week and a half—I still wasn't okay. I remember my parents taking me to the house, and I said, "You know what? I feel like my brain is not okay." They're like, "Aileen, just take the meds as prescribed." I'm all, "No, they're giving me wrong meds."

I think they were giving me like uppers. You know? I remember getting on the phone with our insurance, since I was nineteen, I was still on my parents' insurance. I said, "Give me some doctors in San Diego. Give me a couple in San Diego." It was like none of these doctors in Orange County knew what I did. My parents were like, "Hell no! We are not taking you back to San Diego."

Dr. Michael Lardon was one of the two doctors I was given. My current doctor who's been one of the biggest blessings in my life. He was the only doctor who was honest with me. At our first appointment, he was like, "You fried your brains out." He said, "You are so lucky. You go to the school on the top of the hill, all these crazy kids partying it up." He said, "I have kids in mental institutions that are never coming out. They got to where you are at, but they did not come back."

I've learned so much about the brain and the chemicals in the last twenty years because he showed me all of it on his dry-erase board on that first visit with him. He's like no psychiatrist because he would say things such as, "This is your brain. All your neurotransmitters are going like this." When he gave me antipsychotic medication, he said something like, "This medicine is going to calm your brain down, and it's going to get you operating." My very first thing was, "Oh no, I'm crazy. I'm nineteen. I have to take meds for the rest of my life?" Because that's the stigma.

He assured me, "Just follow a treatment plan. I'm not going to tell you how long. Just follow the treatment." Like anybody that's nineteen and gets told they need to be on medication for their brain, I thought I was crazy. I was labeled crazy. My peers knew what happened to me. My family circle knew what happened to me. I knew I wasn't crazy. I knew that I had just had a huge psychotic trip. It could've happened to anybody, but you don't know that. You don't know what your brain is like. You don't know what drug is going to affect you differently. After learning I was the only one within my group of friends that had a negative experience, Dr. Lardon gently helped me realize that my brain chemistry is different and medical intervention would be my best option."

But yeah, there was an imbalance already. That is really my passion that there are people that don't even know they're imbalanced, or there are people that are severely imbalanced. At the time after the trip, I couldn't even get to baseline. I know that medical intervention helped me. I'm not advocating medicine, but I'm saying, for goodness' sakes, if you are a mental person and if you aren't feeling okay, *seek the help*. Seek the therapy, seek the psychologist. Yes, spiritually I pray that you have faith in somebody. I mean, for me it's the Lord, of course #firstGOD.

PATRICK SILVA. I'm interested in that period when you fell on your knees, and you felt that feeling you were going over the edge and you were going to stay there. Your brain. You were losing your mind. How long did that last? Was that feeling like so overwhelming that you thought you were never coming out, and then did you slowly reduce the feeling to a point where you're thinking you might win this thing?

AILEEN MEZZA. Yeah. I want to say when that happened because it was so vague that they injected me with something because I must have knocked out. I just remember waking up the next day. So I want to say that when I yelled, "It's very fuzzy," that they might have come in, or maybe I fell asleep, or maybe I was already injected. I can't remember everything that happened, but I'm sure they gave me something to sedate me because after that, it goes a little black. I had a little blackout. I remember waking up and going to the bathroom, and I remember them checking me out. I remember—

PATRICK SILVA. So how long were you in that place?

AILEEN MEZZA. That's what I'm trying to say. It must've been just one night. It must've been a twenty-four-hour hold.

PATRICK SILVA. Normally they're seventy-two.

AILEEN MEZZA. I was so out of it that I don't even know. That's what I'm saying. I'd have to go back and see. My doctor must have those records from when that happened to me.

PATRICK SILVA. Had you done shrooms before that?

AILEEN MEZZA. Yeah. I had done them twice before. They were always intense. I loved doing them. It was always like I mentioned before, a lot of people trip on this stuff, and they're like, "Whoa, tripping off—

PATRICK SILVA. Kind of the reflection that we see on TV where they portray somebody on shrooms with the funky noise and the psychedelic sites?

AILEEN MEZZA. Yeah. It was always fun, but it was always deeper. I do believe it was always taking me to like you mentioned before, an enlightening experience. Today, that I'm thirty-nine going on forty, and actually on January 13, 2018, it was twenty years ago this all happened.

PATRICK SILVA. Wow.

AILEEN MEZZA. As I reflected this past January 13th I couldn't believe it had been twenty years.

Today I sit here in awe that it was just last year that I began on the journey to writing this book.

CHAPTER 6

Being Colombian

My parents are Colombian.

Although, I am American, Colombian American. My Colombian roots run deep in my blood. Time after time, I am asked the question, "Why are you so prideful? You weren't even born there." True statement but not 100 percent. I was not born in the actual country of Colombia in the continent of South America. However, I was most definitely born into a little Colombian colony of Colombians in the state of California in the US of A.

I am immensely grateful for the cultural pride I inherited. It is sacred to me and something of great value to me that no one can ever take away from me.

Colombians are happy, fun party people. My family is from a town in Colombia called Barranquilla. It's a coastal city next to Cartagena, Colombia. The city's nickname is *Curramba*. I know this because I grew up listening to songs like "El Carnaval de Curramba" by Cuco Valoy.

My mother and father adore being from Curramba and not just from Curramba but from *El Barrio Olaya*. The people from this part of the country are known to be really extroverted, fun, and wild. They have a carnival that is said to be second to Brazil's. But honestly, I have only heard of that being said by my Colombian family.

What I could tell you is just like any other carnival. It is truly *epic*! It begins on Saturday, *Sabado de Carnaval*, and goes until Ash Wednesday. It is four days of pure partying.

Sadly, I have not been back to Colombia since high school. That means twenty-plus years! To be exact, I went in 1994 during carnival time. What a blast it was! I am currently planning a December trip this year (2018) because I have never been in December, which is also party season there.

Do you observe how many times I mention the word *party*? If there is anything Colombians like to do and know how to do well, it is *party*! Am I proud of this? No! I'm just speaking the truth. Okay, well maybe a little because partying is fun.

My mother and father, they came here in the late '60s. My dad served for the US Army for a couple of years. He was stationed in Korea. He lived in New York for a couple years with his aunt and cousins. We probably would have been raised in New York if my mother would have liked New York. But my mother did not like New York even though my father loved it.

If you ask my dad about New York, until this day, he says he can remember most of the subway stops from Queens to where he worked in the city. My mom just did not feel that New York was the place she wanted to settle and raise a family. Even though my dad insisted that he never planned to raise a family in the city, he desired to move to Upstate New York and settle there.

Meanwhile, my great-grandmother and grandmother were living in Los Angeles, California. So naturally my mother gravitated toward wanting to move to California to be closer to her mom as most daughters do than stay in New York. My parents moved to Los Angeles and got married in Hollywood. I always laugh because they got married in Hollywood, but I don't think they lived there for very long. I don't know the details. Of course, I hadn't been born yet. All I know is that they were hard workers.

My dad worked for Delco Battery, which was owned by General Motors for thirty years, and retired pretty well. My mom worked for Hughes Aircraft which was later bought by Boeing. They moved to the United States from their country like many people. They wanted a better life for themselves and for their future children.

As I'm thirty-nine years old now, I realize that, and I respect them. I respect what they did. But when you're a teenager, when you're a kid, and even when you're in your early twenties, you're still at that point that you sort of resent your parents for being a certain way.

My parents were strict. They overly wanted to control and protect us. They weren't in Colombia anymore though. But you know, they wanted so hard to protect us, and I understand it. Even though they were now in America, they didn't let go of their roots. They didn't just not let them go. They truly embedded them in my sister and me.

We ate, breathed, lived Colombian. Although I loved it, I didn't realize at the time that I was living in somewhat of a bubble. When I was in college at San Diego State and people would think I was Mexican, I would take offense to it, not because Mexicans are bad but because when you have such Colombian pride embedded in your blood, it's difficult to entertain the idea that you are anything but Colombian.

I went to Colombia when I was really little. I actually was baptized Catholic there. However, I didn't go back until I was older, and I currently haven't been back in over two decades. But I still remember it vividly as if I was there yesterday.

Being Colombian is a huge part of who I am. I wouldn't be Aileen Amador Mezza if I didn't have Colombian blood running through my veins. I love salsa. I love merengue. I love cumbia. I speak Spanish. I love the people. I love the food and have a love, passion for soccer. Hence, the FIFA World Cup in Russia 2018 is presently happening. There is nothing I enjoy more than putting on that Colombian jersey and rooting for the Colombian national team as I have been doing since I was wee, little.

This bubble I lived in literally felt like a Colombian colony in California. All I knew growing up was Colombians, my best friends growing up. We were always around other Colombians. It was rarely just my nuclear family as in my mother, father, sister, and I *ever*!

Growing up, there was always a group of family of friends that we all did things together. That included family picnics, vacays, and holidays spent together. I don't think my parents or my mother, for the most part, like doing anything alone.

Even today, I find myself having to explain this all to my husband. He doesn't always understand why I need an entourage; I always want to be with people. I like to bring people together, just like my mother did and still does.

My parents loved hanging out with their friends. They loved partying. They really were party animals. I'm sorry, Mom and Dad, you were. If there's anything I know, it's that Colombians know how to throw a good party.

And guess who were the ones usually throwing the parties?

My parents, they were the type of people that would invite everyone and their mom over to meet up. I know that definitely I took after them in that matter, especially my mom.

My mom and dad loved throwing parties, and they knew how to throw a good party. They were great at catering to others. My mom would always cook up the main dish for the party while friends brought over appetizers and other dishes potluck style.

My dad ended up remodeling our garage into our family room/ party room. He even had a custom-made bar built in. He always made sure he had the music playlist ready, meaning the records, cassettes, and CDs that he was going to play for the party. Sorry, Millennials, this was a time where iTunes did not exist.

I got my love of old classic salsa from my dad. I would always stand around him and ask questions about the songs I heard. He had a passion for old salsa like Hector Lavoe, Eddie Palmieri, Willie Colon, Sonora Matancera, etc. I have his same taste of music until this present day. And during the parties, there were times I took over for my dad playing the music. There is just something about salsa and merengue music that wants to make everyone get up and dance.

That garage was really a nightclub on party nights. My dad even had the colored lights and all. I'm telling you, my parents were all about the party. What did they expect from their daughters? One of the two of us was bound to turn into the party animal as well.

I mean, really? Mom and Dad, you kind of created this monster.

My mom is all about Colombian folklore. Her passion is the art of Colombian folklore dancing. Again, my parents are from Barranquilla, Colombia. Barranquilla is the same city that Shakira (singer) and Sofia Vergara (actress) are from. My mother has been the director of a Colombian folklore group she established years ago in 1994 for the USA World Cup that is called *La Puya Loca*. Throughout the year, she is contacted through her Colombian people networks in Los Angeles about events they would like to invite the group to perform in.

In 2006, somehow, Shakira's people contacted my mother. My crazy party Colombian mama was invited to meet with Shakira's video production team for her upcoming video for the song "Hips Don't Lie" which also featured Wyclef John. My family's partying so hard over the years led us to all debut in her video.

In Shakira's "Hips Don't Lie" video, my mom's group *La Puya Loca*, whom at the time I was a member, all got to participate. The group was compiled 100 percent of our family and friends. I still remember the day that my mom told me that Shakira was looking for a folklore group that is specifically from Barranquilla, Colombia, to act out a real-life carnival scene from the *Carnaval de Barranquilla*. I laughed that day, but then it actually became a reality. That day on the set at Gower Studios on Sunset was like no other.

I remember still laughing because as I looked around on the set, it was all my family and friends. All our years of partying paid off. At the time, I invited my BFF to join us on the set. The only sad thing is that I didn't get picked as one of the main girls like some of the others from the group. It was probably because of my chunkiness.

I convinced my aunt who also didn't get picked to throw on the most beautiful of all our folklore costumes, the garabato dress. This way, we would still be able to be in the live carnival scene in the video. I vividly remember me complaining while we were on break having lunch in the greenroom from shooting the video to my BFF.

ME: This sucks. I'm all in the back. No one is even going to see me.
BFF: Aileen, can you be quiet? Dude, look around, your whole family is here in a Shakira video specifically because you guys are from Barranquilla and party animals.
ME: I guess, well at least I know where I was at when I see the video. The video comes out, right?

And in the very last minute of the video, I think for a milli-second, if I pause the YouTube video, until this day, I can show you where I was at. If you're lucky, you can even see the bottom of my dress as I am dancing. LOL.

So moving on, in essence, I was raised in a fun atmosphere for the most part when we were with our friends. My home life is really vague. I don't remember meals at the table. Early on, I do remember that there was tension with my mother and father. There was a point where my grandfather was living with us.

The only thing I remember is that I was Daddy's little girl. I think I knew my dad wanted a boy so bad, and he never got one, so I purposely went to do things with him that maybe a *normal* little girl wouldn't, maybe like things boys would do.

My fondest memories of my dad were of us going together to the Los Alamitos racetrack. He loved betting on those horses. I never realized why he was betting or why he chose what horse to bet on because I was too little. But I do remember I would try to tell him what horse to bet on.

There was one time I specifically told him to bet on a horse, and he did. The horse ended up winning the race. I don't remember the name of the horse. However, I know that for years, he never forgot the name and number of the horse. I want to say it was no. 7 and Prancer, lucky no. 7.

However, in my later years, that dynamic had changed. I wasn't so much Daddy's little girl anymore.

It's sad to say that I don't remember a lot of family time because it was always a big party.

I don't remember it being just my mom and my dad and my sister. I remember friends of the family that were like family and that until this day I have adopted so many adopted uncles, aunts, and cousins. The weekends consisted of family picnics, parties where the adults danced salsa, merengue, cumbia, and vallenato all night.

While the parents were all partying it up outside, all the kids were forced to crowd in some room together until the party was over. And I'm not talking about just like five kids. I'm talking about like ten or fifteen kids in a room, week after week, playing truth or dare, light as a feather, spin the bottle, house, etc.

I was actually one of the youngest kids, so I wasn't actually allowed in the room with all the big kids. There's a gap between my sister and I; my sister is five years older, and there were a lot more kids her age. While in my age group, there was only about three or four of us. So we were forced to play the normal stuff—hide and seek, freeze tag, Nintendo, or just lie on some couch bored until our parents got tired of dancing the night away.

I enjoyed it for the most part. My father had made a lot of friends in New York when he played soccer, and somehow, all these men got married and moved to California like my father. These people all became like our extended family. I have people I grew up with that I find difficult to call just friends because they were more like my adopted cousins. I consider them family because all of us *children* have known each other since birth.

Now that I am older, I have a different view on things. I get this perception that my parents were not happy together, so it was better to have other people around all the time. I only understand that reality now because that happened to me. Because inside there was a void and I wasn't truly happy, I, too, ended up needing people. I'm not sure if that is a learned behavior or just all I knew. The reality though is that it was what I was raised in.

When I was old enough to leave at seventeen, I left, and even though I was trying to go to school and do what a seventeen-year-old girl going on eighteen does when she graduates high school, I wasn't thinking school. I was thinking, "Oh my gosh, I get to do this on my own. I get to have friends, be on my own."

It was basically a culture shock when I went to San Diego State. I was exposed to people who weren't Colombian, and I think maybe I was just so overwhelmed by the difference. I used my older sister's expired ID for the longest time to get into clubs and buy liquor. I kind of felt cooler than others because I was one of the few of my peers at San Diego State that had a fake ID. Suddenly, I was thrown into this world where I was part of the partying that I had grown up around. I finally felt like it was *my turn*.

I don't think my parents did wrong. I could have listened. I could've. I could've, but I didn't.

I'm a stepmother raising an eighteen-year-old son. It's like a mirror image. I mean, he's a male, but some of the things he's going through, it's like, "Well, I was just there twenty years ago," you know?

I also have a sixteen-year-old son and two little girls, five and three years old.

It's insane, you know?

It's insane.

I realize now that I lived a lot of my life resenting my family because of a bunch of *what ifs*. Children always think, "What if I would've had it like this, what if."

At some point, you have to just suck it all in. You just have to own up to it, and you have to be like, "This was the life I was given. Those were the cards I was dealt." And I could've chosen to do things differently, I could've. But I didn't.

I understand what they were trying to do. They put a lot of pressure on my sister and I to excel in school. And I was, for the most part, a great student, but it all went downhill when I left home and I went to San Diego State.

Because at that point, I wasn't even really thinking of school. I was just thinking, "I'm free. I'm free, out of Victor and Lucy's reign [Victor and Lucy are my father/mother] and all these Colombian parties."

We used to attend parties at plenty of my friends' parents' houses, but our house was well known. My mom and dad loved parties. If they could throw a party every weekend, they would.

There were some Sunday mornings where my sister and I would wake up, and we would have a drunk guy that couldn't drive home, passed out on our couch.

This was my reality.

Also, there were countless mornings where we'd wake up, my sister and I, and there was a foreign man at the breakfast table with us. My parents would always say, "Oh, it's, you know...He couldn't drive home last night, so we let him stay."

Ironically, that's what happened to me when I went to college. I knew how to party. I think partying was just also in my DNA or something.

I mentioned the word *party* a lot being a Colombian. Please understand that when I refer to partying, it's being used in a literal sense. I must make mention of that because Colombians are known to party because of the white powder. I can't be certain what probably did or did not happened at my house because I was so young and naive. However, it would not surprise me to find out today of the things that really did go on there.

I was so naive.

That's why when I got to college, I was like, "Whoa." The real world hit me like a ton of bricks. I just didn't understand it because I had grown up in such a bubble.

My parents were super strict. I have an older sister, and she had issues when we were growing up because she got the brunt of it. She was first. She didn't know how to deal with it. She's also more introverted than I am.

I'm the extrovert, so I was pretty much the happy-go-lucky person.

I don't know what was going on at times internally with my father. I don't know. All I can say was at some point, he took a lot of anger out on my mother and sister. And that's something that he had to deal with. As I look back, I know my dad suffered from anxiety/panic attacks. There would be such heavy fights in our home that we would have to end up calling 911 because my dad would start hyperventilating from his anxiety/panic.

There was definitely resentment from my sister to my father for many years.

We looked like the picture-perfect family, but again, it's all about perception and image. What others saw from the outside looking in, my mother was all about that—the perception of others.

I believe I still focus on my looks, aside from the fact that I gain weight and lose weight (an endless cycle) because of my mother. She has always put high importance to how others perceived us. But I don't blame her. All humanity is about that. I get it now too!

I mean, when you're a woman that's catering a party every week, you focus on, "What am I gonna wear to the party? How will this look on me for Saturday night?"

She just loved us looking great. Looking back, it's sad because it was a false perception. But that was our dysfunction.

Now, because I'm older, I understand it.

If you don't yet, that's okay. You may not understand it where you're at right now. And again, that is okay.

But if you're reading this and thinking, "Gosh, I feel the same way that she felt in her family," I just have a piece of advice for you. Don't hate your parents. Love on them. Ask them questions and ask them to be honest with you. I think the parents that were basically first-generation parents that came from various countries to America just didn't know how to be honest with their children, with you. It's not that they didn't want to be. It's just all they knew how to do.

Don't hate them when they discipline. Discipline is part of being a parent. You simply cannot be your child's friend. You have to be that disciplinary figure, and I learned that after I became a parent myself. I suddenly understood where my parents came from. Sure, they were extreme in their disciplinary methods, but like I said before, it was really all they knew.

And guess what? They didn't do a bad job.

I look at myself, and I see a successful real estate mortgage loan professional who is now writing a book. Of course, it could've been better. I could've had my own MD on the cover of this book, and maybe I will someday. But for now, I really don't think I turned out too bad.

All our parents really want is for us to be happy and successful. We are their pride and joy. I only understand this now because I look at my children and I feel the same way. I feel like I want them to succeed, and I want to do whatever it takes to help them get there.

I feel like perhaps I may have let them down with what happened to me. Ironically, it was my sister who was diagnosed with major depression when we were younger, not me. When we first started seeing a psychologist, it was because of her. I was supposedly the *normal* one.

But what is normal?

All I can say to you about your parents is that you don't really know what's going on or what they're trying to do at this moment. I definitely don't resent mine at all anymore.

I wouldn't change my life or what happened. Everything that happened led me to the point where I am today. Everything *had* to happen in the way that it happened so that I could be right here at this very point right now.

I remember specifically one family vacation when we went to Hawaii. I was four years old. My grandma and aunt went with us as well. We also would take road trips to places like Lake Tahoe, Yosemite National Park, San Francisco, etc., and honestly, those all were great memories I have of my childhood.

As for my daily life growing up, I can't say that it was full of joy. But I wouldn't change it.

The dysfunction was just how we were.

CHAPTER 7

Catholic School

I want this book to be my voice coming to life for the world to hear. I have a story, and I need it to be heard. So here we are in another chapter of my life.

This book came to life with the support and love of so many people, especially my husband who told me to just do it. I just want to take a moment to thank my God because it was through His infinite wisdom, the paths that I was put on, and everything that happened that led us here to this point—my voice on paper, telling my story. Amazing really.

I grew up Catholic and have twelve years of Catholic school under my belt. What does this mean? It's just that my parents really did try their best with my education and schooling.

I went to preschool at Happy Time preschool before I started my Catholic schooling. Such a cute name for a school. I loved it so much that I can close my eyes now and vividly see my classroom, imagine the teachers serving us peas and carrots, and laying down for nap time.

I attended Whitaker School for kindergarten. Whitaker School is part of the Buena Park School District. I lived in Buena Park and was raised there for twenty-six years of my life.

My parents were doing well for themselves, which is why I believe they were able to afford to send my sister and I to private Catholic school. I attended St. Pius V from first to eighth grade and then attended an all-girl high school called St. Joseph High School in Lakewood, California. This all meant that I also had the privilege of wearing a uniform for twelve years of my life.

Since I was baptized and raised Catholic, I went through my First Communion, attended confession, my confirmation, etc. At Catholic school, we would go to church/mass every Friday with the student body.

I recently reached out to my principal from St. Joseph's High School on Facebook. Her name is Dr. Mendoza. I said hello and of course asked her if she remembered me, she replied, "Of course, I remember you. How could I forget you?"

How could she forget me? She couldn't. I was an excellent student, and I was on honor roll almost every quarter. However, remember that my conduct wasn't always the best. Not to mention that I was always tardy. I had to go in front of the disciplinary board a couple times due to my consistent tardiness, so the principal was aware of who I was.

I also got caught cheating. Everyone cheats, but I always got caught. So I had to go in front of the disciplinary board again. At the time, the disciplinary dean of St. Joseph High, Mrs. Nelson, was also familiar with me. I remember many conversations with Mrs. Nelson in her office.

I wasn't a bad student. It was just that there was always something going on. During one of the many times I went to Mrs. Nelson's office, I remember her asking me, "Is there something going on at home?"

Remember, it's all about perception. So my answer to her was, "Everything is fine," except that my sister's bulimiarexia was getting out of control and making her suicidal.

Fight after fight.

It was crazy at home.

But you know, *everything's fine.*

I never had thought that there was a correlation between misbehavior and trouble at home until I decided to revisit these memories for this book.

During my teenage years, on the outside, I appeared to be this smart, outgoing, happy-go-lucky girl. Inside, I was a mess. Everything at home was affecting me even though at the time, I didn't realize it.

The human brain is so amazing. It represses memories and events to protect you. It's just a defense mechanism to help you survive.

Even though I went through twelve years of religion class, I didn't truly understand. I enjoyed getting prepared to go through the sacraments, but I didn't understand. I was so caught up on the rituals and the customs of the Roman Catholic Church, having to go through a priest, that I didn't know if God really loved me.

Twelve years of Catholic school and I was unaware that God is merciful and bestows His grace on all men. I didn't know.

Had I known He would forgive me and that He loved me, maybe things would've been different.

I know my parents did their best by sending me to Catholic school, thinking that I would learn about God and that I would embrace our religion. But at home, we didn't practice.

We didn't go to church on Sundays, only on Easter, not even on Christmas.

Catholicism gave me the foundation I needed, but I was studying and learning about God out of obligation simply because I was going to a Catholic school. Once a month, we would go to perpetual adoration, and the school clergy would put the host up, and we would all kneel down in front of the altar and pray. But you needed to have something to pray for?

God I pray to now is all over the place. I think the Catholicism I grew up with is so caught up on the rituals and the restrictions that I was only focused on that. God gives us a guide, the Bible, and it's meant to guide us, but we are disobedient because we are human.

Since the beginning of time with Adam and Eve, humans have been disobedient. But you know what? He forgave them. That's something we aren't really taught—it's okay to make mistakes as long as we learn from them. We will be forgiven.

God is going to chastise and discipline us, but that's only out of love. He wants to get us on the right path; and everything that

He's done, everything that has happened to me, it was to get me on the right path. All the doors He closed and all the doors He opened, there was a purpose to them all.

Twelve years of Catholic school and growing up identifying as Catholic taught me nothing about the God and the Lord that I pray to now. This may not be the case for every Catholic. But it was in my case. It only taught me about restrictions. Everything was forbidden. I believe that it's only natural to rebel when there are so many suffocating restrictions that close you in.

I genuinely loved attending an all-girls school, and I didn't care that there were no boys there. I feel like it built my confidence up to attend an all-girls school. I valued Catholic school, but I felt like if you're not practicing what you're learning at school at home, then what's the point?

I understand what my parents did, and I appreciate them for it. I love them for wanting the best for me.

Twelve years of Catholic school but it took a lifetime for me to understand God, His love, and His way of leading us to the light.

I started this book with a bible verse (Matthew 7:7–11) that stated, "Ask, and it will be given to you; seek, and you will find; knock, and it will be opened to you. For everyone who asks receives, and he who seeks finds, and to him who knocks it will be opened."

But what does it mean to knock? Are we knocking on God's door? Or are we just asking?

Knock, knock.

Who's there? (You always have to ask who is there before you open the door, right?)

When you knock, you want somebody to let you in, right?

So why should He let you in?

Are you living a life that can be considered worthy?

Are you being obedient?

Are you doing things that are wise?

You want Him to open doors for you, but you're falling short in certain areas?

You can say you pray, and even for me, I used to say that before I found God.

When I got on my knees for the first time willingly, it was because I truly had no choice. I prayed to God to get me out of the darkness.

When I was hospitalized for the first time, I screamed at the top of my lungs for help. What I saw on the wall was a light from heaven, and God told me that I was going to be okay.

He opened doors for me not to stay there. I was doing things I shouldn't have done, and I was stuck in a loop, stuck in a trip that didn't end. The Bible says that demons tremble at His name. And that's what I focused on when I was in that dark place in that hospital. Praying night and day, "Lord Jesus, Lord Jesus, bless me."

The first time I was hospitalized was definitely one of the most traumatic, but it was also the time I met Jesus. I fell to my knees and recited a little prayer card that my parents had given me of one of the patron saints in Colombia. I recited the prayer daily, hoping, wishing, begging for the demons to leave me.

Those demonic presences left me alone, and I was brought out to the light.

I'm not saying that mental illness is just a spiritual experience because it's not. Sometimes you need medicine. But in that particular moment, what I needed was faith, and it was in the darkness that I truly found God.

CHAPTER 8

Identity

My parents are very prideful people, and I definitely get my sense of pride from them.

Although, I know that I need to practice being humble.

There are times where I believe I have a good heart and good energy, but there are also times where this good energy turns into overconfidence and a belief that I am above it all. That's when I know I've entered a manic phase.

I'm able to understand now that I used to go manic and I'd be on this high. I consider myself balanced now because I can catch the signs of the mania and tell myself to slow down. I have to sit and tell myself, "No, you do not have superpowers. You are a human."

Slow down.

I want to believe that this drive comes from my constant strive for perfection. I mean, who doesn't want to be perfect. I'm an over-achiever, so I have always set my expectations extraordinarily high.

But I have learned that while it's okay to have high standards, I need to lower my expectations because I end up stressing myself out and then beating myself up. But why do we strive for perfection? It goes back to perception and what others think about us.

Have you ever done a pro-and-con list in regard to the positive and negative traits that identify you? If your con outweighs your pro, I would say you have some work to do on yourself before judging others. I challenge all to practice doing their pro-and-con list as often as possible. See what kind of leverage you have between the positive and negative traits that make up your true identity. It can help you realize what areas you need to work on building up a better character.

As you are well aware of now, I didn't have the perfect family. But on the outside, we looked like the perfect family. But why would others perceive that? That perception couldn't be more false. We certainly were far from perfect. Were we even happy?

No.

We were a complete mess.

Even though my mother always wanted to paint that picture of the perfect family and people's perception of us was exactly that, I've come to accept that image and what others perceive is not reality.

Every time my mother would throw a party, she would be all up on us on what we were going to wear because she believed that we, her daughters, were a representation of her and thus needed to look good.

I caught myself today arguing with my five-year-old because she wanted to wear a purple shirt with these red and black leggings, and it didn't match. I told her, "No, you can't go out like that. You're a representation of me."

Should I have said that? Was it wrong? Should I have let her go to school all mismatched because it was her choice?

I don't want to treat my children like they are objects or that they are an extension of me. I know that's what my parents did, even though they didn't realize that they were doing it.

Maybe that's parenting. Maybe you are just so unconscious of what you're doing and what the outcome will be. You just pray to God that these little ones will turn out to be okay.

Part of me wants my children to be proud of me and realize the mess that I went through and how it wasn't perfect. I know God purposely placed this imperfection in my life to guide me to where I am today.

He made us imperfect. It's just so hard to accept that it's okay not to be perfect.

I have a tattoo on my lower back.

My tattoo is of a red heart with this bible verse under it, "Perfect love casts out all fear" (John 3:18).

Back when I was in England on a missions trip in 2009, I was full of fear—fear of the unknown, fear of failure, fear of everything.

God is perfect love, and He is the only one capable of casting out all your fears.

I've always feared the worst, and obviously, you cannot control what happens, only your reaction to it. But God is pure love. He makes things perfect, and with His love, if you just submit to everything that is happening and understand that He has a plan for you, in time, this will cast out all that fear.

The process of us being sanctified, going through these trials until we reach our final destination, used to scare me.

But you know what? We're here on this earth, and I am doing the best I can. I pray that God gives me a long life to touch others, be there for my family, but if that isn't the plan, I no longer fear death either.

Don't get me wrong. I want to be around, and I don't want to die. I can finally say that and know where I'm going. I don't say that with fear. I say it with affirmation, and I couldn't always say that.

I'm in a place in my life where I've realized that it all starts from the inside. The Lord is consuming me from the inside out, changing me from the inside out. He does this throughout our entire life.

Every time He's doing it, every time He is consuming us, you're somewhere else in your life. Each day, I'm somewhere else than I was last time He consumed me from within. We are works in progress.

He's not done. My life isn't perfect. But that's what's so beautiful about it.

In my office, I've got a little picture frame that I purchased, and at the bottom it has three little clips to hang photos, and it says, "Your life does not have to be perfect to be wonderful."

The very first picture on the frame is one of my blended family. I have four children and will always say that I have four children. Even though my two eldest are my stepsons, I embrace them as my own.

They're currently eighteen and sixteen years old, but I have known them since they were four and seven. Their father and I didn't actually get together until a while after I met them, but I always did feel a pull toward them. For some reason even prior to their dad and I dating, they always gravitated toward me.

We got married when the boys were eight and ten years old. Life doesn't have to be perfect, but I've got my version of perfect. God has blessed me, and although it's been an additional challenge that I've had to endure for seven years, we have been married thus so far. I wouldn't have it any other way.

I thank the Lord every day, and I look forward to what He has for me in my future.

My life isn't perfect.

But I am blessed.

CHAPTER 9

Living

Happiness is a state of mind.

Joyfulness is ongoing and everlasting.

I try to live life and be happy and joyful.

I'm at the point in my life where I put my faith in God when things are down and remain joyful because I know that He has got a plan. Nobody can rob me of that joy.

I don't believe in luck anymore. I believe that we are destined for things, and while we have dreams, if they're in line with God's will for your life, then they're going to happen. It's not luck.

When I was younger, I just wanted to have fun. I lived for the thrill. I never thought that anything could bring me down. I didn't realize that I was actually a sponge, just soaking it all up.

I built my own little world, my own way of coping to just be happy. I definitely think I went about life doing that. I just ignored it all and went about my life.

In my early adolescent years, when my sister's eating disorder surfaced and there was a lot of turmoil in the house, I tried to maintain that everything was fine with me. I put all the blame of the turmoil on them, disassociating myself from them.

They were crazy.

I was fine.

They were the problem.

My entire family was going to therapy, but it wasn't until 1996 that I was asked to step in and speak to the psychologist they all had been seeing. It was the spring of my senior year of high school, and I had already been accepted to San Diego State. I was introduced to Dr. Vance Becker who later became like a second father to me and ended up as my psychologist for over a decade. On my very first appointment with Dr. Becker, one of the first things I told him was, "I'm the good one. I'm the one that's always okay. They're the problem."

Ironically, it was me who benefited the most from psychotherapy in the last twenty years.

My sister stopped going.

I genuinely believe that had she stayed in psychotherapy, she might have ended up in another place today. At one time, maybe medication would've been needed and beneficial.

But when the topic was approached, I believe she rejected the idea. There is a heavy stigma that hangs in regard to mental health, and too many feel that taking medication is like admitting to actually bring crazy.

It's just that we have to understand that we are human, and that sometimes, things in life get us so down, so down sometimes that we really need help.

And you know what? That's okay.

It's okay to need help.

Two weeks before I began to sit and write of this section of the book, something traumatic happened to us as a nation. On February 14, 2018, Nikolas Cruz opened fire at his former high school, taking seventeen innocent lives, the deadliest school shooting since Sandy Hook. Ever since then, I have been on social media and online reading on all these forums.

The kid was mentally ill.

It's been so heavy on my heart that it's not just the psych meds that make people crazy; it's the fact that resources are not made available to individuals.

If you're able to deal with anxiety, depression, anything on your own with exercise, diet, and holistic meds, then go for it. All power to you.

But the reality of it is that some people cannot even get to baseline; they can't even get balance to where they're able to focus on eating right, exercising, or such. This is the reality of it.

Some people are more off-balance than others.

Sometimes it's just something in their genes. It saddens me that you can treat mental illness in so many different ways, but the one way that is constantly attacked is if you treat it with medication.

And sometimes, the medication itself is the problem. Nikolas Cruz was on medication, yet he still shot up his former school. A pill in itself can't kill, just like a knife or a gun by itself cannot kill. It's a matter of heart and mind and the instability of the person. Yes, he was on medication, but perhaps it wasn't the correct treatment plan or dosage for him. Maybe he was on the right medication, but perhaps he didn't have the right support system or the right people treating him.

In my case, I am immensely grateful for the ongoing unconditional love my mother, father, sister, and entire family always gave me. Even close friends that although they did not understand what was going on, they were there to listen and love. You all know who you are, and for all of you, *thank you*. A proper support system is also key to obtaining optimum mental health.

So...moving on, I, Aileen Amador Mezza, flipped out of my mind twenty years ago and was in a mental institution where I was stuck on a trip for doing psychedelic mushrooms.

My mind went to a realm where the average mind shouldn't go.

I was fighting for my sanity.

It wasn't just a trip on shrooms because I had experienced that before. But for some reason, on this third occasion, I had an episode on them.

You better believe that I prayed to God, and I wish I could've just prayed to God, and He would've miraculously healed me. I wished I could've just gone to a holistic doctor or just changed my diet and exercised.

But you know what? The reality of it is that I did pray. I got on my knees in that mental hospital, and when they closed the door on me, I looked around observing the little window, a steel door, and a little cot.

I prayed to God, and you know what he did? He sent me Dr. Michael Lardon a couple weeks later.

To say the least, Dr. Michael Lardon saved my life. He's the one that educated me and told me, "You fried your brains out, and you're so lucky you're here. Your neurotransmitters are all over the place. All the chemicals, the dopamine levels are skyrocketing in your brain. I need to give you medicine to calm your brain down."

Do you think that if I had just prayed about it, which I did, that God would have healed me in that moment?

I did pray.

And God sent me a medical doctor who had the wisdom and didn't abuse the fact that he was able to prescribe medication.

God led me to Dr. Lardon. That I am certain of.

Another door opened in that moment.

However, there are good mental health professionals regardless of some rotten apples. I am blessed that God sent me the best of the best of psych MDs.

He helped me get to baseline, back to sanity. But do you know how?

Because I agreed to temporarily take meds if he felt I needed to. At the time, he was still experimenting trying to find the perfect cocktail to balance my brain chemistry. I have been on Zyprexa, Risperdal, Seroquel, and I had suicidal thoughts. Because these medications are so potent and powerful, it's best to be educated on side effects and how it will be affecting your body and brain.

Some of the side effects are because they need to get those chemicals balanced, and sometimes—I'm not going to lie—the right one doesn't work, and you have to be patient with it. You've got to persevere. You need God and the medicine.

For years, I believed I was crazy because I had to take the medicine. But today, I know that I would've never gotten to baseline without them. I was so anxious and not altogether when I lost my mind.

The chemicals in my brain felt as though someone dumped a puzzle and never finished putting it together.

But Dr. Lardon helped my neurotransmitters calm down with the right dosage and treatment plan. It makes sense to me. But it might not make sense to others.

I look on social media, and I see people saying, "Psych meds kill." If someone is on a treatment plan with a good doctor for years and is living a healthy and balanced life, you shouldn't attack that person or condemn them for taking medication.

Praise them for embracing their mental illness and taking care of it, just like a diabetic person that chooses to inject insulin into their body. There will be people who tell the diabetic to just change their eating habits, but some people need the insulin.

Heck, some people have high blood pressure, and you know what? They rather take a pill.

Taking medication isn't *the easy way*. Who are you to say what's *easy* and what's not? Stop putting everyone in the same box.

Kudos to those that are able to do it on their own, but don't look down upon those that can't. You're not in their brain. You don't know what's going on in there.

I know what I saw and what I thought.

I have faith. But I know that what brought me back to sanity was medication, along with my faith in God.

Yes, there were times I wanted to get off them due to the side effects. But I persevered and had a wonderful support team. I had an amazing psychiatrist. I had great family support. I had good friends.

Sadly, there are people like Nikolas Cruz who were unaware and were unable to seek the right resources that I was allowed access to. There's a combination of things that are needed to manage mental illness because it is so spiritual and chemical at the same time.

It hurts my heart that some people think that medication is the problem when in reality, it's the abuse of medication that is the issue. It's people not being given the right medication. It's people trusting just the medication and not getting the proper treatment plan.

I needed God, medication, and psychotherapy to get me back to where I needed to be.

Mental illness is genetic, just like diabetes, cancer, and heart disease, and I know that all of these run within our genetic line. I have an aunt that is schizophrenic, a grandmother that had a psychotic break in her young adult years, and my father has always had a bit of a battle with anxiety.

Maybe if I never did those shrooms, it would have never come out, but it did. I'm not weaker because I know the medication has helped me, and I need them.

What is it like to lose your mind? Do you know what it feels like to be on the other side? Are you aware of the chemicals and what they feel like when you're not all together?

My journey with medication has been a series of ups and downs. I've been on and off medication and was even off of them for a couple years until I had my first baby. The hormones and my susceptibility to mental illness brought me to a place I needed to get back on them, due to the fact I was suffering from postpartum depression.

I was off them again, and then my life got overly stressful a couple of years later. But it's okay. I'm a human being that's susceptible to mental illness. This doesn't make me weaker. It makes me human.

Today, I'm on my way to forty, and I cannot say that I have not been grateful to a wonderful psychiatrist who is also a good friend to me now. Together, we want to fight to help those that really do need meds or don't need them to seek proper treatment.

Let us break these stigmas and fight for mental health for more funding to have these resources available to everyone.

One of the biggest, if not the biggest, epidemics today is no longer cancer, but rather mental illness. Look at the number of veterans on the streets, the amount of homeless people that can't deal with their demons, those who hurt others in hope of dulling their pain.

So much needs to be researched when it comes to the brain. I know the place where my mind went, a lot of people go and don't ever come back, and I'm blessed that I came back. When life gets stressful, I get imbalanced, and it's not because I'm weak.

In a perfect world, I could always eat well, and there would never be any stress. But we don't live in a perfect world. There's always going to be stress. There are going to be arguments between my husband and I or with the children. There are going to be times when the children get sick. There's going to be stress at work, school, at home.

So what happens then? Do I turn to a pill?

The medication is always my last resort, and it's not easy knowing that it can get so bad that a pill is necessary. I'm proud that I'm able to recognize when I can't do it on my own and then when I need the proper help.

People ask, "Are you going to stay on them?"

I don't know. But what if I do? Will they kill my liver? Will my lifespan be cut short?

My grandmother died at eighty-seven years old and had a Ziploc bag of seventeen pills that she took every day. Eighty-seven is a good, long life. Did those pills kill her? I don't know. She had been taking them since she was forty years old.

My grandmother was a woman with so much faith. She lived until eighty-seven because she took those pills. She took them daily with faith!

Last year, I decided to get back on medication. Dr. Lardon prescribed my usual cocktail for me, antidepressant (Prozac) and mood stabilizer (Lamictal). At the moment, I thought it was the worst thing to happen to me. I didn't want to get back on meds either for the same reasons people don't want to take them in the first place because of the stigmas. But my husband and I prayed. God gave me the peace and confirmation that I needed the medication again.

I've been unstoppable since then.

I do think about coming off of them as I also think of staying on them, but when will that happen? I don't know.

In a Facebook open forum from a holistic doctor's Facebook page, I once saw a post from a gal that read, "Oh my gosh, I'm going to get off my Lexapro because of what these holistic people are writing." And I thought to myself, "Absolutely not."

In a lot of cases, medication prolongs life.

It's the abuse of medication and the business of big pharma, those that get into this industry because they know they can make money. They push it on the doctors, telling them how much they're going to make. The FDA isn't at fault. It's the greed of man. It's not the pill itself that's harmful. It's the human heart and a man not dealing with his demons.

CHAPTER 10

I Couldn't Wait to Grow Up

I couldn't wait to grow up. What does that even mean? Why can't you wait to grow up?

Because when you're a kid, you look at the adults, and you're like, "Wow, I want to be like them." Every age had its own meaning. The first age that officially held meaning was thirteen because then you're officially a teenager. And then at fifteen, you can get your driver's permit or have your quinceañera if you're Latina.

At sixteen, you're able to drive, and of course, at eighteen, you're considered a legal adult. How many of you could really say you were an adult at eighteen though?

Not me. I thought I was, and of course, I used that line on my parents, but you're really still a kid at eighteen. I thought that after eighteen years of living, I was qualified to be an adult.

It's funny because I'm currently raising an eighteen-year-old right now. I have a great relationship with my eighteen-year-old, and I am thirty-nine right now. I can't believe that I was doing all of this twenty years ago. He pulls out the same cards that I used to pull with my parents.

The only difference is that I graduated high school when I was seventeen, and I turned eighteen in college, whereas my boy is still a senior in high school. So he still has to follow rules because he's not paying rent, not working on his own and still has a couple of months before he graduates.

It's interesting why we can't wait to grow up. Looking back, I definitely could have waited.

There are times when I think, if I could rewind and do things differently, would I have? And the answer is always *I don't know.* Sometimes you think that if you relive your life, you would've done it differently.

"Live your life with no regrets" is a common saying, but to some essence, I think it's not about living your life with no regrets but rather, not thinking about the regrets because there's always, to some degree, regrets. You will have regrets, but you just don't dwell on them.

I don't know if I would've done anything differently, but there lies the problem in human nature; we don't just accept that these are the cards we were dealt and that we did the best that we could.

Maybe it wasn't perfect, but that's okay because it's not meant to be perfect.

Don't be so hard on yourself.

If you are still breathing, if you still have a pulse, there's still time.

You are not done yet.

God isn't done with you yet. It's so important for you to understand everything that has happened to you up until this point in your life has a purpose. I don't mean just take life laying down. Learn from your mistakes. Grow from them.

As a mother, one of the most important things I hope to teach my children is that it's okay to make mistakes. It's okay to be somewhat of a mess because life isn't perfect. Life isn't going to be perfect.

And that's okay.

CHAPTER 11

The Dreamer

I can't tell you how many times I stood in front of my mirror, practicing my Academy Award speech. Ever since I was a little girl, I've always been a dreamer.

I always felt like I was destined for something big. I guess I was somewhat a little narcissistic too. LOL. So I'd stare at myself in the mirror. My daughter does it as well, and I'm sure she gets that from me.

My childhood best friend and I were big dreamers. We used to say that one day, we would ask Oprah to have us on her show. We were both going to make it happen, all while being best friends.

We had a falling out last year, and it hurt me very badly. We had been distant for a while, and I was hurt by this. I'm the type of person that voices things out loud and has no filter when they're hurt. She's the type that represses everything. I know words hurt, and I'm certain my words hurt her, but something happened last year that confirmed that something wasn't right between us.

We had been best friends for thirty-five years. Recently she reached out to me again, and I'm not certain what to do with this. But the Lord works in mysterious ways, and we just have to trust the process.

Back to my childhood dreams, I always dreamed about being something big. I never knew what the big thing was though.

So from a very young age, everything I did I always poured myself into it and wanted to do well. I never had a 4.0 GPA, but I was on the 3.6–3.8 GPA range.

I dreamt of being financially independent, and I know how to stretch a dollar and get money. But I don't budget well.

My biggest dream, though, was and still is winning an Academy Award. However, the dream when I was younger was because I perceived that obtaining fame was so cool. So my dream was to then become a Hollywood actress and win an Oscar. Today, I perceive it differently. I perceive it as being recognized for a work of art. For instance, today I would rather be behind the scenes. Today the dream is more about a best screenplay, best director, production, or movie. Whatever it be, only God knows if I will ever obtain it.

I wanted to be somebody as if I wasn't already, right?

I suppose everyone wants to be somebody. But aren't we all somebody, even if we aren't somebody in the public eye, right?

I think God showed me early on that perhaps I was special, that I had the light inside me, and that there were greater plans for me.

The ironic thing is that I'm not looking for fame. I am putting my life out there, and I dreamed of being very successful. Maybe going back to school? But is that even possible with four kids?

I dream a lot.

Growing up, my sister had this poem book, and she would write poetry. One specific poem of hers was published, it was called "Dreams Do Become Realities."

I just pray that the day I see my dreams become a reality that I am prepared for it.

CHAPTER 12

Spoiled

There is a method to *my* madness.

Everything really does happen for a reason.

At the age of twenty, I had a black Mitsubishi Eclipse Spyder, two doors, super cute, but it was pretty much a coffin I almost died in. I was in a horrible accident where I broke my collarbone and slashed my right ear.

I have thirty stitches behind that ear and an ugly war wound to prove it.

I'm lucky to be alive.

It was a pretty bad accident. My friend was driving and yielding on green to make a left. I was the passenger, and as she turned left, I noticed a white bronco coming straight toward us. Thank God I saw it coming. I reacted quick and actually took my seatbelt off and curled into consul.

Had I stayed in place, I probably would have not made it. It was bad. I've always been quick to react, so that was a good thing in this incident.

The reason I mentioned about this vehicle is because at the time I felt pretty cool owning it. It was pretty rad at the time.

I remember going to the Irvine Spectrum Shopping Mall with my cousin around this time. In one of those vender kiosk, I bought one of those personal license plate frames that said, "I'm not spoiled. I just get what I want."

I remember my cousin seeing the frame and saying, "Oh my gosh, Aileen, that's so you!"

What does it mean to be spoiled? Was I spoiled? Did my parents spoil me, or was I able to manipulate them into giving me everything I wanted?

I don't know.

I never believed I was really spoiled, but rather, if I wanted something, I would go after it in a way to guarantee I got it. Manipulative? Possibly.

Or perhaps I'm just very good at convincing others in helping me get exactly what I wanted. Perhaps on the exterior, it may look like I was spoiled.

It didn't help that everything was about appearance and perception. I had to have the best of the best, and only that, to uphold a certain image. There was a point in my life where I thought I needed to have a Coach or Louis Vuitton purse on my arm.

Now I don't care about it. Just be you. Don't let the label define you.

CHAPTER 13

Mental Health Advocate

I'm not saying get on medicine. I want to clarify that I'm not advocating for pharmaceuticals. I'm here to try to get people to stop putting everyone in the same box.

You can pray, and you may feel healed.

You can go to a holistic doctor, and you may feel healed.

Awesome. That's great for you.

You can be on psych meds, have a great doctor, and you may need them for a season or perhaps even a lifetime.

Everyone is different. Everyone's situation is different. People have this skewed thinking toward medication like it's bad. They're only *bad* because doctors are prescribing them incorrectly. There's a whole business behind the pharmaceutical world, all dictated by money. The insurance companies and pharmaceutical reps give out incentives. Greed is the problem.

There are people that are just doing it for the money, and that's where the bad doctors step into play. I have been able to educate others and have the passion to be a mental-health advocate because I had an amazing teacher, Dr. Lardon.

I'm not on antipsychotic medication anymore, but I used to be. My incident in 1998 was a drug-induced psychosis. I was cuffed and taken into a mental hospital. Had I not taken the antipsychotic medication in that moment, I would more than likely never have come back.

Meditation, prayer, exercise, going to see a holistic doctor—these alone were not going to bring my brain back to baseline. I prayed to God in that hospital, and he answered my prayers by sending me a qualified doctor.

The one and only doctor he blessed with the wisdom to properly treat me. I wouldn't have made it back out. That's why I genuinely believe that my story is so powerful, not because I'm advocating medication. I'm not.

But because there are people out there who do need the help of medication, and that's okay. I am one of them. I'm not in denial I went crazy. Thank God that I had the guidance of Dr. Lardon as well as antipsychotic medication.

I've been talked about by my peers and by my family. Everyone's a little crazy, but I can tell you that when my mind went and came back, I thanked God it came back. It only came back because I stuck to a treatment with my doctor.

I prayed and was one of those people that was adamant against taking medication, insistent that it was only for crazy people.

The reality of it was that without my medication, I was even crazier.

There are people out there that have fried their brains or done some serious drugs. These people can't get to baseline by just simply praying for it. They may have had experience with bad doctors that overmedicate, or perhaps they're on the wrong medication.

I understand that.

That's why my passion is to hopefully provide resources and to help those that want to seek healing, whether by the power of God they are able to be healed by prayer, therapy, or even medication. There is no shame in any method.

Stop putting people in a box simply because you don't understand that their reality is different than yours.

I am so frustrated with this. I had people attacking me on social media stating, "Stop advocating medicine." I am not. I am living proof and a walking testimony that had I not had antipsychotic medication twenty years ago, I would not be who I am today. I do not take antipsychotic medication currently though. However, I have had the need to be on and off other psych meds through the last twenty years. But I have also balanced my life in prayer. I balanced my life with diet, with exercise. Inevitably though, *life happens*, and I fall off the wagon. I get off-balance. You know what?

Some human beings are more susceptible, just like there is a genetic line to diabetes, to cancer, to everything. On my dad's family gene line, we have some mental illness genes. The drugs brought it out or when I get overly anxious, or stressed. Hey, when I had my babies, I got postpartum. I was more susceptible. Was I weaker? Did I not pray about it?

I'm sick of people telling me, "Because you let yourself blah blah blah." Are you in my brain? Did your brain go to where mine did and came back? Where do you people get this bologna? Where do they get that it's okay to take medicine for anything else, but the minute you take it for your brain for mental illness, it's like ludicrous?

Perception is reality.

I don't care if people are going to call me crazy. People have called me crazy for so long. I know God. I know He healed me.

Am I weaker for being on medication? No, I'm not.

I don't care what others say. I feel that right now it's working for me. There's so much I want to know about the brain that I don't care if I have to stay on medication to research that more in depth. As long as right now, it's working for me. I will stay on it. And those who judge me for it, go right ahead. Only God is worthy of judgment. That is what is wrong with this world.

People do not want to be open and seek help.

Why?

They're afraid of judgment. So they live alone with their lows. They don't realize that America's biggest *epidemic* is mental illness.

For goodness' sakes, even Hollywood celebrities, whom all humanity idolizes, find themselves alone. My heart has been broken with all the suicides in the recent years. Just to name the few that impacted me the most are Robin Williams, Chris Cornell of Sound Garden, Chester Bennington of Linkin Park, and the two most recent, Kate Spade and Anthony Bourdain.

What brought them to the point that they felt so hopeless that their only hope was to not exist anymore? The ridicule and shame of admitting they're suffering from mental illness prevented them from being able to battle and fight off those demons we all face.

When will it end?

Have no shame. There is *no shame in my game* because I learned years ago that had I not been open with my struggles, I would not be the individual I am today.

If I didn't tell someone I'm on medication, they'd never know, people within my current sphere of influence know nothing of my history (Well except now they do…lol). That's honestly the goal of medication—to bring you to the operational and functioning level that is considered *normal.*

Every brain is different. Just like when I tripped twenty years ago, I ended up frying my brain, but my friends didn't. I ended up on the street naked and then taken in by the cops to a mental institution. Something in my genetic disposition, in my brain chemistry was different than my friend's. Everyone's different. And everyone reacts differently.

I've never been in denial about anything in my life. I embrace and own up to things. In school, I was a horrible cheater because I always got caught. I wasn't always the best daughter or friend. But I own up to my shortcomings.

People have never been afraid to tell me how they feel about me, and I've had to take it. I've been hurt and been dramatic, but I take it. This is why I don't care about being bold anymore and just letting it all out.

People have often criticized me, and more often than not, it was not constructive. I learned to let things roll off of me like butter. When I was institutionalized for the first time, I was so worried about what people would say about me. Whatever anybody says, it doesn't define you.

I don't deny the wrongdoings I've done in this life. I am not perfect. I own up to it. I shouldn't have done drugs. I haven't been the best human. I have my faults. But you know what?

I try.

I try to do better.

My character has been built up because I've accepted that if people perceive me a certain way, maybe there was something I needed to work on. Maybe the Creator of the universe is trying to tell you that your energy is not good, and you need to work on it.

You make the choice.

Don't be in denial about who you are. Whatever it is, it's okay. You just have to embrace it and make it work for you. Then let God take care of the rest.

CHAPTER 14

Realities

My husband's ex-wife, the mother of my two stepsons, called me earlier this year to talk to me about our eldest son. We are a blended family, and that has come with another additional set of challenges. However, we do our best. She actually has become like a sister and friend in the most recent years. This case is extremely rare. But again, we do what is best for our boys. Getting back to her call earlier this year, she wanted to let me know that she suspected he was suffering from anxiety and depression.

There are things because she's his biological mother; he feels more comfortable sharing with her, and of course, I respect that. And vice versa, there are things he shares that he feels more comfortable sharing with me because I am his stepmom and can bounce to the friend role more easily. However, in regard to this situation, he did let her know that it was okay for her to share with his father and I. At the time, our son was actually open about the idea of therapy. In that moment, it all really hit home with me. He's eighteen and just about to graduate from high school, and that's a pivotal moment in one's life. My prayer was and has been that I can continue to be an ongoing support to him in these difficult years of where you think you know it all but really *know nothing.*

It was in this very season in my life when everything started to change. My home life was mad, and I couldn't wait to escape. Mad in the sense that because everything looked fine from the outside, the maintenance of that perfect image, when in reality, things were not okay.

Being raised in the atmosphere I was raised in was pure madness, craziness from my parents' heated arguments, our Colombian culture, the party scene, my parents being super strict, the issues between my sister and my parents, my sister battling a severe case of bulimiarexia early on in her teen years. On occasions leading her to suicidal attempts and hospitalization, it was like a breath of fresh air to be able to get away.

I couldn't wait to apply to college and finally escape my bubble. However, I wasn't ready for real life. In college, I began to dabble in things that neither me nor my family thought I would ever get into.

I'm grateful that today I have been given this opportunity to pour my heart out, be open about my mistakes, and share my entire experience with the world.

Granted, if I didn't live through that chaos and dabble in things that I shouldn't have, I probably wouldn't have a story to tell. Again, *everything happens for a reason.*

In the end, I can no longer go back in time to relive and change. Those opportunities have been lost. The time has passed; until now everything that has happened has already happened. I have no choice but to own up to what happened and move on.

To some degree, humans have regrets. We all do. I'd be lying if I said I didn't have any regrets in my life. But I don't dwell on them because I realize that every choice, every mistake led me to this point in time right now.

I was raised Catholic. I went to twelve years of Catholic school, the great education I do not take for granted. Catholicism did lay the foundation of who God was for me. However, I really didn't learn how to have a relationship with God until I was forced to seek him with all my might in that mental hospital room in January of 1998.

It's true; it's in the darkest times in a person's life we come to the realization that I do not have it on my own strength to go on. In that moment, I needed God's grace. My deliberant disobedience had led me to a place that at the moment I would not have wished on my worst enemy and still don't.

God met me there, as fallen and lost as I was. All my anxieties, passion, stresses, etc., came out in this shroom trip that could have left me permanently institutionalized had He not given me grace. I speak out because I pray to God that no nineteen-year-old kid experiences what I went through. I did have a conscience. I grew up knowing right from wrong. But it was more fun to play with the little devil on my shoulder rather than the angel on my other. The little devil to me was always more fun than the angel. Who even listens to the angel, right? That is what we do until we find ourself with no resort, so weak and deep in our mess.

If you don't believe in God because you believe it's phony, let me tell you, I did too. It wasn't until I was locked up in a room in the mental institution that I finally found Him. I was on my knees begging for his mercy, begging for the return of my sanity.

As humans, we're flawed and lost from the beginning of time, just reference the story in the garden, Adam and Eve, "The Fall of Man."

Good and evil have existed since the beginning, and while it may all sound phony, it's where my faith lies and whom I choose to believe in.

I could just put my faith in the universe and stars, but I tried that before. It wasn't the universe and stars that I saw on the wall in that room. It was a light from above; that I am certain of. The Creator of the universe and stars came to my rescue. I needed a manifestation of something far greater than a universe at that moment. And until this day, I believe and know I am somewhat of a walking miracle. But was it a miracle?

You see, God knew my heart. He knew that all my decisions would lead me exactly to where he met me in that room that day. This is what I believe: It was my *human will to want to get out of the situation.* When I had nothing else in me, I sought Him with all of my being, and it was then he showed up.

He was willing to give me a second chance. God just wasn't done with me yet. There is a character in the Bible that I often compare myself to, and that is Job. Job in the Bible was a good man and very prosperous. However, in his book, it talks about how God allowed the devil to test him. And throughout Job's struggles to understand his circumstances, he begins to search for the answers in all his difficulties. God ultimately has a plan for your life; that I am certain of. A favorite scripture of mine that is actually taken from the book of Job is "I know that You can do everything, and that no purpose of Yours can be withheld from You" (Job 42:2, NKJV).

Lately, I have observed that there is such a huge population of mentally ill people that make up the majority of homeless on the streets. In the moments I have to glance at them on the street while I'm either driving or walking, as I really get a chance to observe them, there is a particular observation that always comes to the light for me.

Although they seem to not be quite all there, there are many that I silently have heard preaching and looking up to the sky. I can't help but believe these people are just as stuck as I was during my psychosis state, as if they're alive but fighting that same spiritual battle to get out of the darkness in their head and come to the light.

But how can they ever win?

If their brain is so far from coming back, why is that? Because their brain is completely off-balance and way off already. All the neurotransmitters and chemicals in the brain have gone berserk, as did mine when I fried my brain.

Do you know the name of the two most powerful neurotransmitters (major chemicals) that are responsible for the center of all our behavior in our brains? I do.

The answer is Dopamine and Serotonin.

Honestly, I have been a patient of the field of psychology for over twenty years now. #truestory. And although that statement is pretty crazy to admit, I really can't fake the funk. It's my truth.

In those twenty years, I have been treated and trained from some of the best professionals in this field. I am not referencing any book when I share the knowledge I'm about to share with you. This is all coming directly from my educated brain. Today it is the common knowledge I hope to share with you in layman's terms.

Heck, I have spent twenty years researching and studying this field in order to finally come to the conclusion of what really happened to me in 1998. I lament still that even though I consider myself somewhat of an expert in this field, I do not have the PhD, MD, or MFT behind the Aileen Amador Mezza. Hence, that is why the fact that Dr. Lardon's foreword and MD on my cover means the world to me. Because in a world of recognized titles, he has given my story the credibility and validity I have needed to come out of the closet with it.

I digress again.

Dopamine vs. Serotonin in a nutshell (drum roll, please).

Dopamine is the *neurotransmitter* responsible for our *feel-good pleasures*. It's responsible for the euphoric feelings we feel, for example, when we're in love or *think that we are in love*. It is also responsible for our drive and motivation. Lastly, it regulates our mood. So what happens when there is an abundance of dopamine shooting out all over your brain? Basically, you start to get looney, as in my case. Again, I crack myself up. I mean, I have to laugh at myself when I'm coming out to the world as the poster child for mental illness.

Serotonin is the *good stuff* (the angel) we need enough of to maintain a healthy balance to be able to indulge in a healthy matter in our *feel-good pleasures*. LOL. Again, this is straight from the brain of Aileen Amador Mezza, NCR (no credential required). Therefore, when the *bad stuff* aka Dopamine (the devil) wants to come in your brain like a topping on a sundae, the individual loses balance in their brain, and all their chemicals get all out of whack.

And what is the result then? Depression, the demon himself!

So how do you continually cast that nasty demon out?

You tell him you like strawberry instead of fudge. No, silly!

You tell him caramel because that is everyone's favorite. Okay, maybe just mine.

Again, off track. Focus, focus! Aileen!

No, what happens is you need a new remedy because too much of the bad stuff is bad for you.

Hello!

You need an abundance of Serotonin so you can kick that demon out every time he tries to come in with his little minions named anxiety, stress, food, alcohol, drugs, etc. You put up a sign and say WRONG WAY! I don't want to play right now.

This illustration may seem silly, but I am trying to make again some light of the situation.

Serotonin is responsible for depression in the same way that food is *responsible* for hunger. If you have more food, the hunger will go away, but it didn't cause it in the first place!" ("Serotonin—Responsible for Depression?" retrieved from http://www.clinical-depression.co.uk/depression-faq/serotonin-responsible-for-depression/?faq/seratonin.htm/).

Now getting back, the day that I lost my mind, I saw the light, and I reached out to the living God. It's crazy to think that losing my mind, I was able to see things that for some reason I couldn't have ever seen before.

Twenty years ago, God revealed himself to me at that mental hospital. He told me I was going to get better, and even though I wasn't 100 percent, He led me to Dr. Larden. He led me to someone who would treat me and make me better.

As God is my witness, I am good and most importantly *sane* now! Nothing in this life is coincidence, and maybe my purpose was to experience all of this in order to share my story with the world.

As a Christian woman, I did do my due diligence and pray. But prayer wasn't always enough. I am a woman with strong faith, so lack of faith it was not.

If you are that someone in need of medication, do not fear it, please.

And if you're someone who is healing without medication, do not condemn the individual who is using medication. The only one who can truly know whether you need something in your treatment plan is God, and He will lead you to the paths that will open up for your healing process.

I will never deny that. I am living proof that the Lord will guide you. Here is the raw truth about my initial belief towards Christians. I was that girl who thought Christians were weirdos. I thought my sister was odd because initially she was a hyperspiritual Christian. I grew up Catholic, so I always thought my sister and her group of church friends were weird.

#morerawTRUTH #CHRISTIANBROTHERANDSISTERS youmaynotlikethis. There are just some Christians that act self-righteous. Listen up brothers & sisters!! You're not going to lead anyone to Jesus if you're acting like you're better than everyone else. Rather, you should forgive them for being that way. They're also flawed as well. What were Jesus's dying words on the cross? "Then Jesus said, 'Father, forgive them, for they do not know what they do'" (Luke 23:34).

When I started going to Christian church, I remember fellow Christian sister dictating to me what I should wear, for example, things like, "You know, now that you're Christian, you can't wear low-cut shirts." Oh really? Who died and made you king? Oh yeah, that was Jesus, King of kings, not you brother/sister!

I get it! I know why people don't want our Jesus. The church is in lack of Christians that aren't afraid to be *real* so the Christian stigma also is done away with. No, you don't have to be perfect to be Christian, and don't expect Christians to be perfect because we are not! Since I am Catholic by baptism, I will take it way back to religion class.

Fellow Catholic brethren, why did Jesus die on the cross? Answer: to save us from our sins.

Why? Because we are sinners by nature.

And that is why we call Him savior!

So that is bologna too!

Christians admit we need Jesus every day. Because just as he was crucified, we are as well daily. "I have been crucified with Christ; it is no longer I who live, but Christ lives in me; and the life which I now live in the flesh I live by faith in the Son of God, who loved me and gave Himself for me" (Galatians 2:20, NKJV).

"Then He said to them all, 'If anyone desires to come after Me, let him deny himself, and take up his cross daily, and follow Me'" (Luke 9:23, NKJV).

And what do these two scripture verses reveal?

That is, that it takes *daily dying to self* (our flesh, the devil in us) to be His follower. And to take up our cross means *the cross we have to bear here on earth*.

Time after time, people get this so wrong.

Disclaimer again, remember the part that I mentioned in the introduction of this book? I'm no Holy Roller! I don't consider myself one. However, I choose to *roll with Jesus*. What does that mean? I believe he lives in me. He rests in my heart.

Believe me, I am so glad he knows my heart better than I know it because emotions run wild in there. We're all feelers. And feelings are fickle. God knows it's because of how ultrasensitive I am about getting my feelings hurt that I have had a lot of the drama in my life happen.

Not a Holy Roller! I do roll with Jesus though.

Hence, the reason that this chapter references so much scripture is because I can't speak about Him and not back it up with His word.

When I first started attending Christian bible study, I was adamant about the following.

They say Jesus is your best friend. So like I ask all my best friends, "You want us to roll together?" And if so, you have to take this Aileen as she is. You hear me, Jesus? And You said, "Come as you are."

Reaching out to God is an act of spirituality. Let the Holy Spirit be the one to lead you and tell you if you need anything or anyone else. He will convict your heart of those things that He believes you must be broken of to live the life he has prepared for you.

Time and time, he has proven to me that Aileen must decrease so He will increase in my life.

Man, I am as stubborn as they come. In fact, before I met my husband, I had a beautiful romance with Aileen Amador. I loved that crazy chick. My life was all about *me*. It revolved around *me*. Everything had to be about *me*.

One of my best friends told me once before getting together with my husband the following:

BF. Aileen, you know why Julio and you are not happening?

ME. Yeah, because he is dumb, and he can't see a good thing when it's staring at him right in his face.

BF. No, because Aileen is in love with Aileen. And until Aileen breaks up with Aileen, God could not give you what he has for you.

In fact, God didn't bring us together and create *the perfect love* that only He could have created until it was time.

Below is a poem titled "Perfect Love."

It's by an unknown author. My husband actually gave this poem to my two best friends and I the first year we met when we were just mere acquaintances. I know this all sounds kind of cheesy. It took three years for my husband and I to finally get together. This poem I always kept in my bible. It tells the story of the process needed before God presented my honey to me, my perfect love. It may be similar to yours or not. If it is or it isn't, it doesn't matter at the moment. Read it and have hope that if you desire a companion still, God knows that, but it's #Godfirst.

The poem ended up being on the front of our wedding invite.

> Everyone longs to give themselves completely to someone, to have a deep soul relationship with another, to be loved thoroughly and exclusively, but God to a Christian says, "No, not until you are satisfied, fulfilled, and content with giving yourself totally and unreservedly to Me, with having an intensely personal and unique relation with Me alone, discovering that only in Me is your satisfaction to be found. Will you be capable of the perfect relationship that I have planned for you? You will never be united with another until you are united with Me, exclusive of any other desires or longings. I want you to stop planning, stop wishing, and allow Me to give you the most thrilling plan, existing one that you cannot imagine. I want you to have the best. Please allow Me to give it to you. You just keep watching Me, expecting the greatest things; Keep experiencing the satisfaction that I Am; Keep listening and learning the things that I tell you. You just wait. Do not be anxious. Do not worry. Do not look at the things you want; You just keep looking off and the way

up to Me, or you will miss what I want to show you. The one I have for you is ready (I am working even at this moment to have both ready at the same time) until you are both satisfied exclusively with Me and the life that I have prepared for you. You will not be able to experience the love that exemplifies your relationship with Me. And this is the *perfect love*. And dear one, I want you to have this most wonderful love. I want you to see in the flesh a picture of your relationship with Me and to enjoy materially and concretely the everlasting union of beauty, perfectness, and love that I offer you with Myself. Know that I love you utterly. I am God. Believe, and be satisfied." (Unknown)

And that was all so very true. I was very much a narcissist of sorts. You see, that is the nasty and ugly side of me, the cross I must bear while I am here on this earth. "For we do not wrestle against flesh and blood, but against principalities, against powers, against the rulers of the darkness of this age, against spiritual hosts of wickedness in the heavenly places" (Ephesians 6:12, NKJV).

I will wrestle with my ugly nature until I am in the heavenly realms. It was never meant to be that your Christian life is perfect. It just means that I am more aware of why things happened to me and will continue to happen if I don't stay on track. "These things I have spoken to you, that in Me you may have peace. In the world you will have tribulation; but be of good cheer, I have overcome the world" (John 16:33, NKJV).

Although it did take dying to that ugly Aileen prior to God bringing my husband and I together, that ugly Aileen is still in this mold. I will wrestle with that nasty part of me forever. The difference is that I am wiser now.

"The fear of the LORD is the beginning of knowledge, but fools despise wisdom and instruction" (Proverbs 1:7, NKJV).

I was a very big fool all those years, and frankly I still am foolish at times. However, today I know how to practice the gift of discernment. I recognize my right from wrong. And most importantly, I know my boundaries and limitations.

But I realize that everything that works for you will not work for others. God has designed us in such a way where each of us is different. It's such a beautiful thought really.

I'm not expecting you to all immaculately become Christians after you finish this book. However, there is a CDROM, sinner's prayer, and a Bible that could be mailed to you on the last page. *Not!*

I thought that was funny. Coming to God is an act of spirituality. You have to allow the Holy Spirit to do the work. I know firsthand I hated people shoving church and Jesus down my throat. The only thing I can say is please don't wait until it's too late like I did. Learn from other's mistakes if possible.

The overall treatment plan that worked for me might not be the custom, tailored one for you, your family member, or friend.

As for those who judge and say, "Well, if you didn't push your brain so hard, you wouldn't need medication now." You know what? If you didn't eat bad, you wouldn't need insulin or have to take heart medication. If you didn't stress yourself out, you wouldn't need high blood pressure medicine.

At the end of the day, who cares if you have to take a pill for your health?

If it helps you, who cares?

CHAPTER 15

The Madness

I definitely wasn't prepared for the real world when I left home. I perceived my home life to be a madhouse, so in essence, when I went away to college, all I was focused on was escaping. At the same time, I had no idea what I was about to encounter.

I love my parents; there's no denying that, but when I left home, I harbored a lot of resentment toward them.

Now, back to… What was the encounter? So, I knew drugs were out there, and I knew people did them, but I didn't realize how available they were. The first thing I remember about moving into my dorm room is my dorm mate putting these two big ole'posters on the wall, one of a marijuana leaf and another "I love Tupac Shakur." I was like, "Whoa, people really smoke weed."

Soon I began to attend the college parties where people were constantly smoking out of bongs, and pipes, etc. Drinking was something I was familiar with seeing, but marijuana—I had been exposed back when I was fifteen while visiting my cousins in Florida, but this exposure was like no other. One thing is for sure I wasn't focused on my education. The only thing I was definitely focused on was my freedom.

San Diego State is known to be a very diverse university, and its reputation for being a party school doesn't fall short. At seventeen, what did I know?

I am going to divert a bit. I was exposed to the workforce during my junior year of high school, I learned then how easy it was to make money if you just worked hard. My high school girlfriends would laugh at me because I would spend all my free time working. I hated being at home, so working and making money seemed like a great idea. I was working for $4.25/hour (which was minimum wage at the time) at Chuck E. Cheese's, and that gave me pretty decent spending money during high school.

I was familiar on what it took to make an hourly wage and how to get paid. I wasn't oblivious to that. I was more in shock with how commonly these college students did drugs. Everyone did it.

I went through the whole D.A.R.E. program during my elementary school years with their slogan being "Say no to drugs," but according to a press release by the program itself, the program actually magnified the curiosity in children and thus increased drug use during older years. Perhaps because of those cheesy videos we watched about drug abuse and use. And here I was, a freshman in college, seeing everyone around me recreationally using drugs like it was no big deal. And to them, it wasn't. That was just how their reality was.

I wasn't prepared. In retrospect, I should've focused on school, but because of everything that had led me to that point, my focus was elsewhere. And honest, it is something I still lament. Early on in life were instructed to follow the steps laid out by society, being, you go to college, get a degree, and perhaps also obtain a higher-education degree like a masters or doctorate. Because, that way people would then perceive you differently.

This world does perceive you by the titles we hold or do not hold. I will say it again. I didn't want to tell my story until I had a respectable title to be placed before or after my name. I felt like my story would be heard or respected more if I had the title. Foolish me, but it's *real*.

The fact that I'm coming out and telling people I went crazy is only due to Dr. Lardon telling me to write it and that he'd endorse it. The book has his MD on the cover because at the present time, I don't hold any fancy title. The fact that the world recognizes the title MD gives this book and story credibility in the hopes that my message will be heard globally if God were to allow.

Moving along, my story continues.

After my drug-induced psychosis, I was forced to leave college. At the time, my sister was working in the mortgage industry back in 1998, and that business was bumping. So two weeks after being released from the mental hospital, I felt the need to do something. I needed to keep using my brain. And so my sister and one of our cousins pulled some strings and got me a job as a receptionist at a big-time mortgage lender at that time, Ditech.

I didn't even know what a mortgage was at the time; fast forward twenty years, and here I am, a mortgage professional *still*. Go figure; I was not in the right mind when I chose this industry. LOL. Nah, just kidding. As much as I hate the stress that comes with it, I actually enjoy it as well.

Anyhow, I was offered the position as a switchboard operator. My shift was a 6:00 a.m. to 3:00 p.m. shift. It was me and this other gal that were on the morning shift only.

Remember, I had just gotten out of the mental hospital a month prior, and there I was, operating a switchboard, answering the phone with the jingle, "Hello, 1-800-71-FIXED."

JP, the gal in the morning shift with me, was an immense blessing in that season of my life. We would spend a whole hour alone before the next receptionist clocked in for the 7:00 a.m. to 4:00 p.m. shift. She sure got a kick out of my story. Imagine your first day of work, and you meet this chick telling you her story that she just got out of a mental hospital because of a shroom trip gone bad.

She was in disbelief and allowed me to always vent out to her for that hour. You see, venting is my outlet. I probably sounded crazier because all I ever did was talk about it. But I couldn't help it.

It's what I needed to do. Had I not been open, I probably would have overdosed on some drug by now or even committed suicide. Although, I was never really suicidal like having an actual plan, but the dark thoughts were there. God knew I needed to work and get those chemical juices in my brain going so that Dr. Lardon could figure out the perfect cocktail in my brain at the time.

JP, thank you for those countless morning talks in that Ditech switchboard room. God put you there in my path too, and I have no doubt. Love you, JP. XOXO.

I realized people were making a lot of money in this industry. And Ditech was a company like no other. I observed how easy it was.

Here I was at nineteen, and I got exposed what it was like to make good money. Today, twenty years later, I have worked for several companies in this industry. I don't consider myself a mortgage expert because there is always room to learn, but I have definitely gained a lot of knowledge and perspective. There's really no other business I would want to be in.

I hold an active California Department of Real Estate (DRE) license as well as a Nationwide Mortgage Licensing System (NMLS) license. However, I have always been quite the mathematician and numbers gal, so my majority of years in the industry have been on the mortgage financing side. However, today I began leaning towards the real estate side.

I was just like any other kid; I was excited at nineteen to be in the real world, but I was vastly unprepared. That's why here I am at thirty-nine years old, still trying to finish a bachelor's degree in human development at Hope International University's online program.

My hope is that after twenty-two-plus years of beginning my college education, I will walk one day and obtain at the very least my bachelor's. I'm a senior in college taking one class every eight weeks. I had to slow down because I was pushing myself really hard last year to try to graduate, and I had all these plans to apply to grad or medical school this year, but the stress got to me.

I was starting to feel like I could actually go crazy again.

I could hear God telling me, "You're going crazy again. You're pushing yourself too hard. Who said you need a grad or medical degree right now to write your book?"

These thoughts were real. And I was made aware that I needed to take a step back. My hope is that with this book, I am able to just pass along my knowledge. I want to let our young adults and all people understand what's out there so that they don't go into real life unprepared and succeed in this rat race.

I have no choice but to just live. Everyone copes with life, and life did scare me. There's power in me coming out and letting everyone hear my story because I want others to know that they aren't alone. Everyone has their own story. So be willing to share yours too.

CHAPTER 16

Losing Myself

My story continued. So here I was, seventeen and a half years old, being exposed to drugs, sex, and the whole shebang. I loved everything about San Diego State. Most of all, I loved the city, and I still do.

The most thrilling feeling was the college life I was living. As shameful as I am to share the following, I must, but that thrilling ride led me to lose my virginity in my second month in college at the age of eighteen years old.

It actually happened on my eighteenth birthday too.

My BFF was pounding on the door telling me not to do it while in the middle of a college party where I was plastered. This story is sad but again very true. I did end up in a huge obsession over the guy because well of the obvious, he being my first.

I mean, come on, isn't that what all crazy chicks do? Go psycho over her first when he rejects you afterward?

From losing my virginity to having to share a shower with all the girls on my floor in the dorms to having a meal card and buying whatever food I wanted to crossing the border into Mexico whenever we felt like it, *I loved everything I was living and experiencing for the first time*!

I was on the ride of my life! I began living the life I always dreamed of in San Diego. And there was nothing I hated about it until it held the awful memory of that incident in 1998.

I never actually completed a degree at San Diego State, but I will always consider myself an SDSU Aztec. Actually, the colors of SDSU, red, black, and white, are my favorite of colors to wear and coordinate. I was blessed to go to school there, even though I was only on campus for less than two years. I felt like I lived there for years because all my friends stayed out there, and despite all the drama with the aftermath of my incident, I was probably out in San Diego every weekend for years consistently while living back in Orange County to pay visits to my friends and party.

The thing that always tripped me out the most though was that drugs were so readily available. I tripped out on those shrooms, and it was fun. It was fun until it got too much for my brain to handle, my emotions on the drugs, the relationships, the friends, the girlfriends, and all the problems. I wasn't even thinking at the time. I was just living.

At SDSU, I had gotten accepted as undeclared major, so the first two years were really just to focus on my general education classes before really focusing on a major. So there I was, this bright-eyed youngster, thinking she was going to major in the freedom of life at that moment.

I look at my son who just turned eighteen, and inside my head, I'm thinking, "Oh my gosh, you just don't know. You think you're ready, and you don't know anything."

The drugs were something else. I had so many good trips, and the euphoria was just amazing. I wasn't necessarily a drug addict, but I had definitely lost control. I was just living to satisfy myself, and I had forgotten what I was created for. I had forgotten that I had a purpose.

I knew that I was going to do something big, that I had a purpose. But during those years, I put it to the side and just lived. I remember growing up with movies where there was a little angel and a little devil on each shoulder, and I can only imagine my little devil ecstatic with my decisions during my years at San Diego State. The little angel on my shoulder was probably like, "I've been constantly telling you to follow your dreams and to know your desires, and you choose to do this? Okay. Go ahead. God's going to test you."

I know that's why I lost my mind. It was a huge test. Those dreams he instilled in me as a little girl were going out the drain. But here I am, twenty years later, dreaming and living in full effect. And as much as you would think I would like to turn back the hands of time. I really wouldn't, I'd leave it the very same. And I'll take the ride I am on now because now I know where I am headed.

Now, in regards to drug use, there are people that can party and do drugs, without taking them to the deepest level I always did. But, does it make it still okay, I am not going to answer that, because it goes back to playing with the little devil and little angel. However, there was something in me, always tickling me, telling me I shouldn't be doing this. But I kept doing it.

What ended up happening is that I tripped so hard that I think God let me taste what it was like to play with the devil. I'm not justifying my actions, but maybe, it was supposed to happen so that I could wake up. Things could've been different, and I definitely cannot dwell on what's already passed.

I could've been better, but I wasn't.

Sadly, this is all sums up how I ended up wandering the streets of San Diego, naked, covered only in a blanket, out of this world, stuck on a schroom trip that could have left me permanently in a mental asylum. But God had different plans, thank you Lord, you met me in my darkest hour, and have redeemed me. Amen.

CHAPTER 17

The Real Estate and Mortgage Loan Industry

I mentioned that my sister got me into the mortgage industry when I was nineteen years old as a switchboard operator, shortly after being released from the hospital.

Now twenty years later and I'm still in the mortgage industry. I love that I'm able to make my own hours, but my phone is on me twenty-four hours a day so that I am available to my clients, in-house processing team, and real estate partners.

I started off not even knowing what a mortgage was and moved from a receptionist to an escrow assistant to a processing assistant and then to a loan processor. Two years had passed, and by then, my sister had left Ditech.com and was now at a job at a company no longer in business that went by the name of World Savings initially. Then it was later bought out by Wachovia and later Wells Fargo. The year was 2000, and I had made an attempt to return back to SDSU. However, it also didn't go as planned. Something upon my return back to San Diego triggered a second breakdown. I returned home again and began working at World Savings as a loan processor.

So here I was at twenty-one years old, making about three to four grand a month, and it came fairly easily to me. I didn't understand the stress that was involved because I was still in an entry-level processing position. I started to see those around me and realized that I could go out and generate my own business and take the leap of faith to become a loan representative. In my eyes, that was a very important position, and I knew the money that could be made from it. I was still at World Savings & Loan at the time, and I was a great loan processor but was always intrigued by the crazy dynamics of all the parties, positions, and most importantly stress that came with the job.

Once I started to go out into sales and taste the money that came with it, I still didn't understand why the loan officers would get so stressed out. To me, on the outside looking in, it seemed like a fairly simple job. It's not rocket science. But I would see these loan officers stressing out because they just didn't understand the process.

There are so many people involved in a real estate purchase transaction, from the receptionist to the escrow assistant to the processor, the underwriting department, the loan officers, the real estate agents, etc.

But I began to realize how all these people hold these different positions, but they get stressed out because they don't understand the process. I've been blessed to know the process because I worked my way from the bottom up. I don't stress as much anymore because I've been doing it for so long. I say that *I don't stress as much*. Keyword is *as much* because this business is stressful no matter what.

However, what does stress me out is the lack of faith in the operations of any lending company. I mentioned the two first companies I ever worked for—Ditech, and World Savings. I can honestly say their business model was close to flawless. Both founders of those companies implemented a system to streamline the processing of a loan like no other. In the twenty-plus years, I have yet to find any company that meets the caliber of operations for both those companies. My respects to Paul Reddam, the original owner of Ditech, and the Sandlers, the owners of World Savings.

I know that I can't get to everyone and everything all the time. At the moment, I am doing what I can as a real estate and mortgage professional. I've managed to maintain pretty consistent production numbers in the midst of so many other projects I am continually working on and diving into. The most important thing to me is my mental health. I've mastered what it is to maintain good mental health. And I am sure you have heard the following before: *You can't put 100 percent of your efforts 100 percent of the time on only one thing.*

I think people sometimes get this perception that I live the most carefree life. I don't though. On any given day, I challenge anyone to do a ride along with me. Remember that Facebook is really Fakebook, so what you see is not always reality. That also goes for a lot of other things. On Facebook, you will see me out and about all the time enjoying life at my leisure with family and friends. What they don't know is that right after that Facebook post, or whatever, my phone is probably in my hand or not too far from me because my job requires me to be available 24/7. I mean, I'm financing houses, not delivering babies, but it's still something that requires full-time commitment.

In the year 2005, I incorporated my own mortgage-services company. I started the company initially out of my home office in Corona. Later I moved it out to Los Angeles. The name of the company was called Prestige Mortgage Services, Inc.

It is no longer in existence because I fell back into my old ways heavily between the years of 2000–2006 because I got a taste of the money. So guess what? I started using cocaine because I thought that my brain could handle it.

Yeah, what a joke.

In my head, I think I believed that because I can do coke and not go crazy in the literal sense of the word that now I was able to hang and be down again. Because somehow, the fact is my brain could not handle the shrooms, not even weed, which actually never was my drug of preference. Frankly, I only did it because it was there or because it helped me come down off the coke the next day.

So there I was, making crazy bucks, but 100 percent of my life was dedicated to mortgage loans and partying. That is enough to make anyone go crazy. I also tried to hold a relationship that was so catastrophic because I lost my very best friend at the time because of a guy who I allowed to come between us; in the end, it was so not worth it. But again, what is done is done. And in hindsight, I got what I deserved by hurting my best friend and downplaying my wrong.

The reality was the people at Ditech were making crazy money in 1998; the people at World Savings were also making crazy money, all the subprime lenders that are no longer in business, all the brokers, all the realtors, and not to mention all the unlicensed people in the business making tons of money.

What is the root of all evil?

Answer is, *the love of money will destroy you and your relationships.*

Money is also the devil. People will kill, hurt, commit adultery, etc., all in the name of not just *love* but also the *love of money.*

So today, I choose not to do that 100 percent.

I strive to maintain a balance of spending that 100 percent broken into different fractions of time. That is focusing on #firstGOD, family, friends, my health, and work. Pretty much in that order is also my hierarchy. Things can wait.

This comes from the *Chicken Soup for the Soul Series No. 47: Think Positive*, "Life is not an emergency."

So don't make it one. Hence, I am guilty of this at times still. It's a constant battle. And if you're in the real estate mortgage loan industry, there is no way around it.

All came down in the fall of 2006 when I had my last and final breakdown and was forced to shut down Prestige. I blew $250,000 of my parents' investment into my business. The previous year, I had reported over $450,000+ to the IRS, at only twenty-six years old of age. Certain that I would continue to rise and make this money, I convinced my parents to take out an equity line of credit of $250,000 against their beautiful home in Corona, California.

The intention was never to dip into it but to simply have it available for cash reserve. Well, guess what? Business started to take a turn for the worst, and I began to dip into it. I dipped into the last of it while in denial that my business was in the red and going under. I truly kept believing that I can give my company a turn around and never laid off any of my employees until the end when I went crazy for the last time in the fall of 2006.

The year 2006 was the year I last used cocaine and the year of my demise. Left with nothing, I closed the doors to my office on Wilshire Blvd located near Koreatown, moved back home to Corona with my parents, and all I would do is fight with my father about losing the $250,000 and try to justify why.

There really was no justifying why. I was partying my brains out living up in Los Angeles, moving from Studio City to in front of the Grove in Los Angeles, spending money like I was some Hollywood celebrity, dating a guy that at the time was probably just as mentally ill as I was but destroying a beautiful friendship that I will lament losing for the rest of my life. You see, that guy was my best friend's ex-boyfriend, whom I knew she was still madly in love with.

I really wasn't in the right mind during that time. I was again living for the thrill, so dumb.

The worst of it all? My mother and father lost that home, partly due to the shift in the market but mostly due to the 100 percent liquidation of the equity line of credit funds, all because of their crazy daughter. Believe me, I have reaped what I sowed.

So now, you see how dumb I was.

It didn't end at nineteen years old and that shroom trip either. I kept living this destructive life with the same patterns. I was insane. I own up to it! I gave people room to talk.

However, had I been more aware and as educated on what I know today, perhaps I would have thought twice before playing Russian Roulette with my brain. I remember having to be placed back on antipsychotic medication after being honest with Dr. Lardon about the fact that I was doing drugs again. Then I would stop doing drugs for a bit, take my medication, feel better, sniff some lines of coke, stop taking my medication again for days, then take them again, then do coke again, drink, party again, etc.

It's like I began to live up to being Colombian now, right? What a joke and such a disgrace to be proud because my family was from the land the purest powder aka cocaine comes from. It destroyed my life. No matter how good of a high, your high will never be as good as the first time.

Dr. Becker used to tell me, "You keep chasing the high and feeling you experienced the first time you did it. That is why you can't stop." What I didn't realize is that that high was a synthetic high. It wasn't reality. It was just destroying me more and more and making me look even more like a crazy.

So many real estate and mortgage loan professionals that get into the business get into it because the money is good, but they get so stressed out because they can't control the transaction and don't know the process from A–Z. The whole mortgage and real estate business is a bit insane; despite it all, I do love it. I would never get out of it because I love the initial contact I have with the clients.

It's my favorite and what I am best at—connecting with others. I love to sit, talk, and learn about them. I love educating them about what it means to purchase a home and how to make that a reality. Even if the time is not now, I will hold their hand until it is their time. And will give them the road map to what it takes to achieve homeownership.

Currently, I am still both a real estate and mortgage loan professional. My passion and vision is to continue lending the helping hand to anyone that comes referred or is put on my path. There is nothing I love more but to help others.

So in 2006, I had my last mental breakdown. I've had three big mental breakdowns, my first being in San Diego at the age of nineteen, the year was 1998. The second was in 2000 when I attempted going back to San Diego. There were too many triggers still in San Diego, and I went into a big panic attack. Then again, my last was in 2006, when I owned my own brokerage and was partying it up too hard in the Los Angeles scene.

Those three psychotic episodes led me to have to be hospitalized overall in five different mental hospitals when you count the county mental hospitals I first was taken to then later transferred out of.

Here I am, baring this all to you, not caring about the judgment but rather praying that you take my experience and use it to guide your choices. If I am able to help just one person because of this, then my goal would have been achieved.

Life after psychosis is a little like being a hypochondriac. You freak out, afraid you might lose your mind again, constantly wondering if and when the next trigger will happen.

I can't help but to feel this way because I got a taste of what it's like to be on the other side, and it's terrifying. I never want to get there ever again, and I would honestly do whatever it takes to stay on this side where there is light. I would never wish it upon anyone. God has blessed me with a taste of it so that I can warn others about it.

You get to a point where you are so worried about losing your mind that you can't get it together. And that's where faith comes in.

When I got lost in the psychosis on the psychedelic mushrooms, I knew somewhere in my mind that I would find my way out again. While I was not okay, I knew to some degree that when I was thrown into that mental hospital, I knew I would get out. I prayed to God. I was locked in a spiritual battle for my sanity.

The worst part is, I was so scared, yet the staff at the mental institution treated everyone in there like animals. Can you imagine mental patients being treated like animals at a circus?

In 2011, there was the story of Kelly Thomas, the homeless schizophrenic man who was killed by six cops in Fullerton, California. He basically was beaten so badly that he ended up drowning in his own blood and was in comatose by the time he arrived at the hospital. He died five days later.

My heart hurts and still aches because I can only imagine what he must have been battling in his mind; I know that he probably was so scared and vulnerable. The way the mentally ill are treated in the United States is so humiliating.

I experienced it firsthand, the mistreatment by the cops when you get taking in 5150 and then the abuse at the hands of the staff at the mental hospital. These places lead you to believe that you're even crazier than you actually are.

So what's life like after psychosis? A constant vigil for triggers. My number one trigger, which I have not been near in almost over a decade, is drugs. I have not had a psychotic episode since the last time I was heavily into drugs.

I was never an addict, but I definitely didn't have control.

My last episode in 2006 was definitely not the worst. The worst was definitely my first time and then the second time. But all of them are just so crazy, and I never want to go back there; that's for sure.

I didn't know that using drugs would set off the mental illness that I didn't even know I had. Had I never done drugs, maybe I wouldn't have had a psychotic episode. That's why I'm here to serve as a warning to kids and young adults who know that they suffer from anxiety, depression, stress, or have some sort of mental illness in their family; stay away from drugs, please.

There's a lot of things you shouldn't be doing, but drugs for sure is on that *no-no* list.

I do allow myself some wine and the occasional cocktail, but I am always wary about the potential aftermath. I listen to when people close to me say something like, "You've been drinking a little too much wine lately." Because even if there is a one out of ten chance that it'll trigger me, I don't want to take that risk.

Lately, my love for espresso shots also causes me to become a little neurotic. I jokingly say it feels like liquid cocaine for me, trying to limit my intake as well these days.

I embrace the fact that I suffer from mental illness similar to a diabetic or someone that has to watch their blood pressure. My life hasn't been easy, and I'm still in the trenches, but I want others to know that there's hope. I'm just like you, and *there is hope.*

People see me and think I've got it all together, but I really don't. I will always tell you that I'm right there with you in the trenches and will be there until my dying day.

Mental illness is not something that can just be cured. It's something to be embraced, something that I have to watch carefully, but it is not a weakness, and it most certainly doesn't define me. It has only made me stronger.

It's not about the ending because we all know that we are all going to die. *It's what we do from now until our journey ends that counts.*

CHAPTER 18

Crazy Chicks

All girls are crazy chicks, but I may just be one of the craziest. We as females are just wired differently, and we all just long to find that guy that accepts your version of crazy.

However, my thoughts are that men tend to be a bit more prideful. But don't get me wrong, we're also prideful, hence, I know it's a huge stronghold I still battle with. But females, they're capable of being a bit more fake and phony. Perception is very important to women, which is why it makes it easy to paint a false picture and keep it going.

I'm at a point in my life where I'm about to hit forty, so I just embrace my crazy. I've learned to live and manage it. My crazy doesn't define me.

I admit that I am a crazy chick, and perhaps that makes me even crazier because who wants to be called crazy? My story and what I've been through make me not like being called crazy, but it is what it is. I mean, if it walks like a duck, talks like a duck, then it must be a duck.

I married the love of my life, but it's not marital bliss. I love and truly adore him. I think he's the hottest man alive, but wow does he drive me insane. You would think that because of our love story that I adore and worship the ground that he walks on. He would probably agree with that. I wanted to be with him so badly, and it took three years before we finally got together.

Eventually the honeymoon stage is over, and you are forced to live with this person for twenty-four hours of the day, wake up with him, sleep with him, clean up after him, etc. I look at the girls that are single, and I know for a fact that it's not something I want to go back to. Sorry, no point intended either.

I think there's something about single women who feel like they're imposing when their girlfriends start to get married. Nobody makes them feel like that, and I feel like I always have to call up my single friends and remind that I'm not dead and that we can still hang out.

Something just happens when you get married that nobody talks about. Your friends change around you, especially your single female friends, and while they don't admit it, you wonder the reasons why.

Women, take heed; you become who you are with. Women, we aren't always nice; in fact, we can be very mean, and for some reason, when there is a group of women feeding off of each other's energy, they are even more catty.

You're not going to like everyone, and I've had people be mean and phony. I can't be fake, but I can be civil. Even if we don't jive, I will still be polite. It's crazy because years back, I had an incident where I tried to be civil and ignore this negative female coworker, and the more I would ignore her, the more she would try to be fake and want to be friendly.

Females don't want to be ignored. They want to know that you're giving them your attention. It's all so dumb. But then, I realize that there is something in that soul that's not happy. You just have to understand that you can't please everyone, and it's okay if some people don't like you.

CHAPTER 19

The Mental Illness

Call me bipolar, manic depressive, crazy, whatever. Your perception of me is your reality and is not mine. Your perception does not define me. That is why I named this book *Look! This Is the Way It Is*. I know that looking from the outside, your perception is what you see and how you interpret it, but it's probably not the reality of it.

I mean, even though I was taken into a mental hospital and have been labeled *crazy*, I've done pretty well for myself. After everything that I've been through, I'm doing the best that I can.

Ever since my incident twenty years ago, I witnessed how people changed around me because of what they thought they knew. I saw it happen with my peers, my family, even my friends from high school and college. I feel like I was written off as crazy.

I experienced psychosis, and even though I didn't know why I was mental and even twenty years later, I can't help to think that people think back to that incident and tie together all of my actions, up until today. I just want to shout out, "Look! This is the way it is. This is the way it's been. Okay?"

I didn't know how to deal with certain things, just like anyone else. For some reason, I'm wired differently. Everyone is wired differently. I finally said to myself that I'm coming out of this and sharing because nothing anybody thinks about me or has said about it defines me. Even though it hurts that people are mean to me because of a perception they have, I have come to understand that there will always be people like that. There will always be gossip. There will always be someone that can look you in the face and then turn around and talk badly about you.

We're not perfect. We're not.

We're all fallen people.

You're not better than anyone just because of the car you drive or the brands you wear or the titles you hold. At the end of the day, in front of the eyes of God, we will all be judged the same.

I've lived my life thinking that I have this crazy label simply because I was taken into a mental hospital. I was the one that had the story told about her. I was the girl that didn't get to get her sorority letters with her girlfriends even though I was the one that initiated it all. I was the one that was *crazy*.

Now I understand why I was acting crazy, bipolar, and manic, and it was due to my lifestyle. When I was living this crazy life doing drugs, I was not okay. I realize that now, but no one could tell me that at the time. A lot of the time, we don't understand that everything is happening for a reason. Do you really know why it's happening? I can finally tell you that I now understand why.

My husband has definitely made me a lot more bold in the last almost seven years that we've been married. Looking back, I was somewhat of a pushover my whole life. People think I'm strong, but I really was a pushover, another false perception of me.

With my friends growing up, especially in high school, I was always the nice one. I didn't get out much. I ran for class president every year and lost every year. I really did.

I kept running. And I kept losing. I just wasn't perceived as popular enough to be voted as class president. Ref. "And, when you want something, all the universe conspires in helping you to achieve it" (Paulo Coelho, *The Alchemist*).

Certain moments in life can never be lived again, like my high school graduation, one moment in time forever etched in my memory. This book is also one of those moments. Here we are, the journey of telling my story, and we are nearing the end.

I honestly don't care what anyone thinks after they read this book because the reality is that everyone is a little bipolar. I don't think I'm bipolar, but rather, I only act bipolar when I'm not really embracing the fact that I have bipolar tendencies.

I go full bipolar when I'm not watching my triggers and doing drugs. But it doesn't define me. It's not who I am.

Your perception is your reality and is not my reality. People always assume that if it looks like something, then it must be it, judging a book by its cover. But that's not the reality of it.

Here I am, putting myself out there, and honestly, it doesn't matter what anyone thinks. I know that I have learned that just because someone looks a certain way that they are a certain way, as I've been on the receiving end of assumption.

All my life I've been chubby, and even though I've had times in my life where I thought I could be considered *thinner* (#truestory), then I go to show my husband photos, and he'd burst my bubble every time and say, "You weren't thin. You were still chunky." And my little bubble would pop. LOL.

A couple years ago, I did this really strict detox cleanse, and I lost 40 lbs. Even then, I was not at the smallest I had been. However, I had just gotten to the heaviest I had been, so I was very proud of the weight loss.

Sadly, I didn't maintain. I gained back the majority of the weight.

Recently, I tried to do the detox again, and I lost 18 lbs. this time. Then I saw someone that I hadn't seen in a while. I was like, "Hey, I lost 18lbs." And they were like, "Really? So you were a lot bigger before?" They couldn't tell that 18 lbs. was shed off of me, and this really opened my eyes to their perception of me.

I know it sounds crazy, but once people view you a certain way, that's their perception of you. It's almost like they can't take off those lenses, and it's so sad.

It's like, "How much weight do I have to lose so I'm not considered chubby, fat, or whatever Aileen anymore?" The answer is 0 lbs.

You don't lose weight because of the fact that you want others to perceive you differently. You're supposed to do it *for you*! You lose weight when you have the proper mind-set.

Again, who cares what you weigh?

You should care for reasons that are not all vain. For me, I know it's an ongoing quest for me. But as I approach forty this year, I know now more than ever I have to get myself in gear. I haven't worked out consistently in years. I'm looking forward to sending my manuscript off to my publisher soon so that I can rest and work on my overall health. And that health includes physical. The mental health is intact, so now I can move downward. LOL.

I always think about how kids don't want to play with the ugly or chubby girl or guys not wanting to date the chubby girl, and I get sad.

I was one of those girls that rolled with all types of chicks, bigger, smaller, same size, etc., girls that were really wholesome and girls that weren't so wholesome. I have literally felt men look at me in disgust compared to some of the other women I was around. Or vice versa, they looked at my friends in disgust compared to me.

It's all so sad because you don't know what that person is going through, and you never know why a person might have all this weight on them. And it just breaks my heart that people just judge people simply by appearances.

It's wrong.

I think that's what's wrong with society and why so many people are bullied these days because people make assumptions, and what they perceive to be reality is what they believe to be the truth. It hurts.

I have felt what it feels like to be really heavy, and I read somewhere that the most attractive people aren't necessarily the thinnest. It's those that actually are average. But then again, beauty is in the eye of the beholder.

True confession, it may not appear that I do, but the one thing that still does depress me is my weight. It's a constant struggle for me. It's that cross I have to bear daily. I get really down on myself because of my weight because I don't feel like I'm the perfect size.

However, then I am uplifted because in my mind, I think I'm sexy. That's all that matters, right? Oh, and what God and my husband thinks.

I've been in spaces where I've been judged, and I think everyone has been. I'm hurt seeing that people have looked at me and assumed things without really knowing. There is just so much pain and it's been tough, so much pain in being looked at in disgust and being looked at as crazy.

I get you. I get people that are hurt.

I had to grow and learn that all of that didn't define me. In fact, the way that you get judged by others defines them more than it defines you. No one should make you feel less than you are.

Nobody.

CHAPTER 20

Christian Church

The very first Christian church I called my home church was Calvary Chapel Costa Mesa in California. The years I first attended I was blessed to have been taught under Pastor Chuck Smith, founder of the Calvary Chapel Movement. Pastor Chuck passed away in October of 2013. The current Senior Pastor is Brian Brodersen (Pastor Chuck's son in law), and his wife is a dear friend/mentor, Cheryl Brodersen (Pastor Chuck's daughter). Today I am blessed to know them both on a personal level. I'm immensely blessed that I have always had their support while on this journey. You see, Cheryl Brodersen was the very person that gave me the opportunity to share my testimony for the first time in 2010 at Calvary Chapel Costa Mesa's Spring women's retreat. After sharing that first time, I felt a tugging on my heart, I knew God had a plan. However, he still had me on the journey that led me to the present. He opened the door wide in so many ways confirming the writing of this book. My husband and I actually met at a young adults' bible study at their church in 2007. The young adult's ministry was called *The Intersection*. The loveliest Canadian couple ran the ministry, Pastor Lorenzo Smith (Lead Pastor, Collective Church, Culver City, California) and his wife Isabelle LaJoie-Smith. I developed quite a bond with those two. And presently are close friends and dear to my heart. Lorenzo and Isabelle have supported me throughout this project/journey of writing my book as well. They have always been so *real* with me, and their support during my first years of attending Christian church was immense.

Digressing a bit again to prove a later point, I want to share the entry below from my journal the week after Easter Sunday of 2018:

This past week has been especially difficult for me because I went off my Lamictal because I noticed a skin rash developing. I had severe hypochondria because of it. I felt like I could really lose it again. I felt off-balance, and it scared me. I truly thought I was going manic, or maybe I was already but didn't know.

I was scared. But I'm so grateful that I have the Lord and that I recognize what it takes to be balanced. I constantly feel like because our adversary knows me and because he tried to take my mind twenty years ago in that mental hospital, that I am constantly fighting that same demon. I'm constantly praying to the Lord to please filter out those thoughts that leave me so scared that I can't move.

God is everything, my Lord and Savior. Without Him, I would not have been able to cast away those demons from me in that mental hospital two decades ago.

It was only Him that brought me out of the darkness when I could not comprehend where I was. Ref. "And the light shines in the darkness, and the darkness did not comprehend the light" (John 1:5, NKJV).

It is important to recognize when something is a spiritual attack, you have to be able to be like, "No, I've been here before, and you're going to get away from me." This week was especially trying because I wasn't really able to function. I started questioning why and asked God, "Why do I need meds?" And He gently reminded me, "I gave *you* this story. That's why."

I need to be on meds in order to serve my purpose. This week, I was reminded that I truly am bipolar at times. But that's okay because I embrace it. On the outside looking in, nobody knows I struggle with these bipolar tendencies because I don't act bipolar 100 percent of the time anymore. LOL. Well okay, maybe 50/50, 80/20, 75/25, 70/30. It just really depends what life is throwing at me at the moment and how I choose to cope with it. I mean, I act a good crazy most of the time. Ha ha ha.

Bipolar is a word used so very lightly to refer to someone that is acting *crazy*. So might I say that I'm a good bipolar now. This whole darn world is bipolar if you ask me.

Interjecting to dissect the meaning(s) of bipolar disorder illness according to Merriam Webster's Dictionary:

Definition of BIPOLAR DISORDER: any of several psychological disorders of mood characterized usually by alternating episodes of depression and mania—called also *manic depression, manic-depressive illness.*

Definition of MANIC DEPRESSION: a mental illness in which a person experiences periods of strong excitement and happiness followed by periods of sadness and depression

Webster did not have an actual definition of *manic-depressive illness.* So what I did was breakdown the root words into three different definitions of *manic, depressive, and illness.*

Definition of MANIC: affected with, relating to, characterized by, or resulting from mania. For example, had a *manic* personality, his *manic* work pace.

Definition of DEPRESSIVE: (1) tending to depress, (2) of, relating to, marked by, or affected by psychological depression. For example, *depressive* symptoms, a *depressive* patient.

Definition of ILLNESS: an unhealthy condition of body or mind.

So basically, the two words that pop out at me are *manic* and *depressive*, then of course that word *illness.*

Hence, I'm okay then. The words bipolar, manic depression, and manic-depressive illness do give a name to my behavior at times. Now am I always acting this way? No way! I would be known as *crazy*, wouldn't I?

My reality is that I do again have tendencies to behave this way. So what I can conclude is that I am mental a lot of a time and suffer from a so-called mental illness. *Illness* is an unhealthy condition of the mind. So you see, it's in the mind. Grab a hold of your thoughts. Embrace the good ones and bad ones. Examine when they come in.

There is another bible verse that I love referencing to go through the process of examination of my thoughts. Meditate on these things: "Finally, brethren, whatever things are true, whatever things *are* noble, whatever things *are* just, whatever things *are* pure, whatever things *are* lovely, whatever things *are* of good report, if *there is* any virtue and if *there is* anything praiseworthy—meditate on these things" (Philippians 4:8, NKJV).

Allow your thoughts to go through the questioning process of Philippians 4:8. Then *meditate on them.* If not, please throw them out. Pray about them. They're then of that adversary that is trying to get you down.

I know I'm not an expert or have an MD or PhD. But although I am not proud of it, I have been a mental/psych patient for twenty-plus years. The only reason I am sane today is because of that same reason. There has been no shame in my game. My life has pretty much been an open book whether I wanted it to be or not. That is why I write this book with no fear of judgment at all.

You see, like it or not, the truth is people will judge when you're *up,* when you're *down.* And I am pretty prepared what is to come after the publishing of this book. It will never stop. And in the bigger scheme of things, *it does not matter.*

People will hurt you; people will talk and talk. Be aware, you do it too. Life is too short to live your life *for reals* dwelling on that. Because those who value *you* won't. They won't assume things that aren't true. They won't cut you off when you tell them your truth, your perception of things. They will take it, which is not always *easy.* This I know, *the truth hurts.* I can be firm in saying this because people have never had a problem telling me the truth. It sucks to hear it, but I have taken it. And I hate no one. I have cut out no one in my life because of what they have said. I accept it even when I disagree. I can't change their opinion of me, but I can change how I react to it.

People are another one of my biggest triggers. My mother and father being at No. 1. Until this day, I am a loaded gun around them. They trigger me to want to explode and *bam!* The trigger gets pulled. Until present day, it still happens. That is my reality.

My husband made the greatest analogy about my relationship between my parents and I. Because whether they like to believe it or not, I am the baby. We three are all pretty codependent of one another. In fact, enabling to a degree. I have to realize that they're like my opponent most of the time when we argue.

My husband's analogy, because he loves soccer so much, is about a team preparing to play an opposing team that is aware of the other team's strategy. You study the team and decide that it is better to play more of a defensive strategy for the upcoming game because you already know how they play.

From now on, I'm using that approach with my parents because *illness* equals unhealthy. And I don't want my mental health to suffer from something that I could have avoided and prevented.

I get it though. You may have people that do the same to you. But try really hard to practice what I share. Accepting and being aware is half the battle.

Now back to that journal entry.

All I know is that God has orchestrated every step of this book. This book has happened so very organically. It started as a dream many years ago, and today it is in execution mode. However, there are times that I think it's me. What does that mean? That I don't want to write this book to boast about it and gain recognition. My prayer throughout this journey all the time is that God will humble me through the process.

The only focus on me is the fact that I needed to write it for healing and the obvious which is the story of *me* being told in first person by yours truly, *me*. I try not to focus on what could become of it. However, at the same time, I am human, and I am flesh, so there's a huge part of me that is terrified of the outcome. I just need to trust in the Lord and his infinite wisdom.

In the beginning of my journey, when I first met Julio, my husband, I thought Christians were a little weird. My sister became Christian first. But she was always so over the top that I didn't see her as all together. I didn't see someone with a perfect life. And whenever I would get involved in the church, I would see a lot of judgmental people.

In February of 2009, I decided to leave and move to Hollywood, Florida, with my aunt and grandmother who at the time was suffering from Alzheimer's. It was perfect timing because I truly was tired of the judgmental Christians from the young adults' ministry I had been attending at the time. By this time, I had had the opportunity to get really plugged in with also other ministries within the church. For one, I began to take mission trips with the church.

My most memorable missions trip with the church was to Millstat, Austria. I actually had traveled there the summer prior to moving to Florida. On that missions trip, I met a pastor that I heard teach and loved his style. His church was actually out of Florida. So it was perfect that I decided to move to Florida in that season because I was able to attend his church. I felt like his message really revealed how human he was. He shared it all so raw, genuine, and with no filter. I felt like, "Yes, finally! A pastor that *really* gets me." His message never made me feel like I couldn't be the Aileen God designed me to be. Sure, God is the potter, and we are the clay. So I did need some resculpting in many areas, but ultimately I remained *me*.

So upon arriving in Florida, I figured I'm going to go visit his church. This pastor really made me feel like I can do this whole Christian thing. I loved it. I served and worked at the church. He had an amazing restaurant with real good food on the grounds of the church. I had an amazing time and season working as a server at the restaurant on church grounds. It was a ministry in itself.

I had left California at that time because my current husband but not my husband at the time (Julio) was getting involved with dating someone in the ministry that I knew was obviously not for him (because, well, we ended up getting married). But before he ended up being mine, he ended up dating somebody that God had already shown me that would put him through that test. That person wasn't for him, and I knew it, but I couldn't take it. You know women's intuition. Don't ask me how, but God had revealed three years prior to my husband and I getting together that he was the one.

There was a lot of gossip and division going on within the group, and the girl that my current husband was dating at the time had really befriended me during that season as well, knowing that I had intense feelings for Julio. He really wasn't into me at the time, but I knew that one day, he would be mine. *Crazy!* I know. LOL. But I knew. Ha ha ha.

It does sound insane, but God had really shown me. It all caused drama, and I left because I just couldn't handle it. I told the pastor that it was messed up that Christians were like this and that I didn't want to be a part of it. And so off to Florida I went for ten months.

I would have stayed in Florida, but the weather just killed me. I learned again that I could be me and still love God, that my God isn't a killjoy, but rather, He lets you be. I was raised Catholic, so I always knew right from wrong, but it was different this time.

There are all those altar songs, one of which says, "Come as you are." But you get all these Christian brothers and sisters that start judging you if you're not walking the fine line.

I had come to the church, and you know, I used to be high on drugs with people most of the time, so this was different. These people were high on Jesus, so what's the worst thing that could happen?

I had one of my best friends at the time tell me that this is what I needed, that I had been spending all my time with my friends partying using alcohol and drugs, so the contrast was what I needed. During that time, I would still go out and have a drink here and there, but I would feel so judged if anyone were to find out about it.

Everyone has different conviction, and I really felt like I didn't want to go to church because of the negative energy. But I realized that there are times in my life that I can't do stuff on my own, and that's why I found myself lost in that mental hospital twenty years ago. I didn't have the strength on my own to get out of the mental hospital.

It wasn't until I got checked, and I had no choice but to say that I can't do this on my own that I reached out to God. I'm not the perfect Christian, but neither are you.

When I say neither are you, I'm talking to the Christian who's reading this and acts like you live behind a picket fence because you are not leading people to our Jesus that way. You need to be *real*. You need to be transparent. You need to say it's hard to be a Christian.

It hurts that time and time again I've heard in the last twenty years people talking about me because for example if they saw me talking back to my mom and dad. "She's being disobedient because she went crazy."

One time, someone I had met at church was working with an old family friend of mine. It was crazy because the first thing that close family friend of mine told her was that, "Oh you know, she's crazy."

I do some crazy stuff, but I'm not crazy! That's a reality. I had a really bad shroom trip in 1998 when I was in college, and I let that shroom trip define me. Just like we let things define us, and that defined me and destroyed my life for so many years. Nobody has walked my shoes but me.

I know I'm not crazy because would a crazy person be able to do the things I do today? I am a successful mortgage and real estate professional. I have four kids. Yes, I have four kids, two that came out of me and two that I am parenting and I am raising. I am writing a book. I'm an entrepreneur. I'm trying to still do school. Am I crazy maybe because I put too much on my plate?

That's not any crazier than the other person. I embrace that I'm crazy. I'm not any crazier than the girl who's super mean to everyone.

It's so easy for people to just write someone off as crazy. But you don't know their story. You don't know anything.

I do want to tell people how important it is to have faith, especially when you're struggling from a mental illness, especially with how cruel this world is and how mean people can be.

You need God.

And in those times that you fall short, those times that life sucks, you don't have it in your own strength. I spoke a lot about how even when I was going to church, I was judged, and I wasn't *holier than thou*.

There was some Christians that knew more than me and so what? It's sad; it's really sad that people even within the church judge. They turn off people to going to church.

What about Catholics, and what about this? I don't care. See, people think that Christianity is a religion, and it's not. It's a relationship with God. Religion is the Lutheran, Catholic, etc. That's organized religion. Christianity's not. So the Lutherans believe in Jesus Christ; the Catholics believe in Jesus Christ. I just want you to know that I believe He's the messiah. He's the one that came to die for our sins; that's all. If you choose to get involved and go to organized religion, that's fine. I don't. I have a relationship with God, and I practice Christianity, which means I believe in Christ.

I don't overspiritualize my faith. He's who I've prayed to since I was a little girl. I was raised Catholic. It's the same Jesus. I do believe, to some degree, maybe because it wasn't practiced at home. I wasn't taught what it was to have a relationship with God. I knew He existed, but the God I learned about at Catholic school, I would pray, but didn't know that he was a God of mercy and grace. Now I know all about His mercy and grace, and oh how it makes all the difference.

I'm not bashing Catholicism because I am Catholic at heart. That's why I'm Christian because I was raised Catholic.

Being Catholic introduced me to Jesus. I just choose not to practice Catholicism. My belief is that it is not necessary to say five Hail Marys or go confess in front of a priest. I don't. There are certain things I don't think I need to do. I could go straight to God and do that. And if you do that, that's fine. I'm not telling you not to. I'm telling you I just hope that you're not one of these Catholics that just goes to church on Easter, just goes to church on Christmas because what are you really doing?

Do you go to church every Sunday? Because I do. For the most part, I do. I mean, I miss days. I'm not perfect. People want to say that Christians are hypocrites. There's hypocrites all over. People are going to judge all over. But in reality, where is your heart? That is all I'm saying. Easter is not about putting on a pretty dress and the Easter bunny. Christmas is not about just Santa Claus. That's the reality.

Is that all we want to teach our kids?

In Colombia actually, they don't say Santa Claus, they call him El Niño Dios. You know what El Niño Dios is? Little boy Jesus.

Jesus. He's the one that brings those gifts. And I think that's beautiful. It's a beautiful thing because that's who we celebrate at Christmas.

Who do we celebrate at Easter? That same baby Jesus that came to live here and died on the cross.

We are a lost world. We are. And I could not have done this life. I could not have been writing this book and putting myself as the poster child for mental illness and saying, "I went crazy." I went crazy, and everybody knows it without Him.

If you know me or knew of me and my name comes up in conversation for some reason and you are an acquaintance or whatever, you know she went crazy. You know she's crazy. That's Aileen Amador. Aileen Amador Mezza. That's me.

I could scream at the top of my lungs and could say, "I am not crazy."

Because I have God in my heart and because He redeemed me, He showed me what went wrong in my life. He showed me at a cost, a very ugly cost.

Having to be in a mental hospital, to be ridiculed, and to this day, having friends and family who call me crazy.

My God told me, "I met you there. I have a purpose for you. That is why you're here today." And that's what He wants to do for you.

Nothing that people say about you defines you. Let it roll off of you. Nothing in this world defines you. You make that choice. And you know who helps you? God. So let Him guide you.

CHAPTER 21

Marital Bliss

I married the love of my life, and it's not marital bliss. I went to hell and back with this man, but we don't pretend. He doesn't pretend to be the perfect husband, and I don't pretend to be the perfect wife.

My husband isn't very fond of this chapter. He thinks I'm turning people off to marriage. I'm not. I'm not turning people off to marriage. I'm telling you that I have a huge, crazy love saga with my guy. Everybody thinks it's short of a miracle he actually ended up marrying me.

My husband's a jerk. Is yours? Or is he a sweetie pie? Is he always a sweetie pie? No. My husband's a jerk. He's a jerk. But he's a sweetie pie too.

I love my husband. But I'm crazy and not crazy in the context of the fact that I have all this history. No, I am crazy. And all men are jerks to an extent.

It all started with Adam and Eve.

I feel like they were hanging out in the garden feeling good hormones going crazy, putting fig leaves on because they were naked. And God said, "You can have any fruit, any fruit, but do not take from the tree of knowledge, the one that's in the middle of the garden."

I can totally envision Julio and I in the garden right now, and I can see my husband as Adam and myself as Eve.

And I can see myself as Eve thinking, "Hey, let's just have it." That's just how I am. It's funny that my parents were always like, "Your friends are bad influences."

135

I'm like, "No, actually I'm a bad influence, Mom. I'm the one that's like, 'Come on, try a line of cocaine for the first time. Come on. It's fun.'"

Seriously. Me.

So back to the garden, "Let's just have one, babe. Let's just have a piece of fruit."

It's funny how men might know what's right, but they'll listen to us anyway. They don't really wear the pants. They follow along because that's who they are.

So Adam and Eve sin, and Adam says, "God, it was the woman you gave me. She made me do it."

My husband did not like me when we first met. He didn't like me for probably the reasons that a lot of other people didn't like me because I'm obnoxious. I'm loud. I'm annoying. I like to talk about myself. At the point where he met me in 2007, which was less than a year since my last breakdown, and all I talked about was owning a successful mortgage business in Los Angeles, losing the business, driving a Lexus that was about to get repossessed.

All I did was talk, talk, talk.

Initially, we had a connection, and I knew we did, but out wardly he wasn't physically attracted to me because I was at my heaviest then. I was at my heaviest plus being on antipsychotic meds. Antipsychotic meds give you that puffy heaviness. It's really weird to explain. I could weigh two hundred pounds today and not be on antipsychotics and still not look that puffy.

Even though on the outside looking in, he wasn't physically attracted to me because men are physical, I was used to being Aileen. I was used to getting what I wanted. I'm a very determined and driven individual, and there might be girls like me out there, that think I'm a good catch. How can you not want me? Okay, you're not worthy. You're not worthy of me. Fine. If you don't want me, someone else is going to want me. I know, women, we tend to do that. It's like a defense mechanism.

Rejection sucks, and he rejected me for three years.

Something in my heart, I don't know, call me a witch. I don't know. I didn't put a spell on him. I just knew, and I just knew he was being a jerk. He wasn't physically attracted, and men are physical. But you know what? I wasn't attracted to myself either. I was mad. My ego was hurt like, "How do you not like Aileen Amador? Come on. I'm Aileen Amador." I pretty much go after what I want, and I think, for the most part, I'm one of those people that attains what I want. But when it comes to love, you can't. It's psycho. It literally is psycho to force somebody to love you, right?

I don't think I ever forced him. I don't know. There was something innate in me that knew he would be my husband, and as crazy as it sounded and as much as he rejected me, I just knew. I see it now, and today, now that we're married, I think God was preparing us for our marriage, for where in my marriage, I'm not going to get what I want. No matter how much you love this person, it isn't marital bliss. It's not about your needs. Most of the time, it's about dying to yourself. It's literally about not your needs. It's about being completely selfless, not selfish.

I met my husband at a young adults' ministry called the Intersection at Calvary Chapel Costa Mesa, which the pastors there were pivotal. They were this Canadian couple that I love, and they were pivotal, pivotal in me staying in Christianity, becoming a Christian because I was able to always be open and honest with them about how I thought Christians were weird. My hubby was one of those persons that I thought was over the top, and I always felt he fit into that group.

It was a young adults' crew that people came at a little self-righteous if you didn't know the Bible, and I just thought it was phony, right?

I expected because he was Christian that it was wrong of him to remain a jerk. I always expected that, "Oh, gosh, you're so mean. I'm telling you let's go have coffee and hang out like brother and sisterly love because we're Christian brothers and sisters."

He would be like, "I don't care if we are Christian brothers and sisters. I don't like you, and I'm not going to go have coffee with you."

"Oh, you're so mean. You're not being a really good Christian." I feel like because I met him at the Christian church, he was held up to a higher standard, and the fact that he was a punk made me so upset.

The fact that he was still human and the fact that, at the time, he was entertaining a girl in the group that I didn't feel was his fit, and I knew wasn't his fit, and at this time, this specific woman, girl was actually befriending me, and I had shared my heart about my hubby Julio today being on my heart, and somehow, there was an attraction that developed between the two of them, and I was devastated. Devastated because for whatever reason I already knew, right? I didn't understand why it wasn't happening, but I was saying something like he wasn't physically attracted to me, and I think a lot of people would say that's shallow today, but I can honestly say I don't think I was whole.

There was some shallowness on his behalf, because men are physical. It hurt me because I knew we had a connection, yet he chose to entertain this other gal in the group because on the outside looking in, at that moment, she was physically more attractive, and it hurt me tremendously. I sat there and watched it happen in my face, and I thought, "Wow, Christian or not, guys are guys. Guys are punks. They're all about visuals. I know this guy loves me, but right now, I don't look cute. Right now, it's been a year since my last breakdown. I'm on antipsychotic meds."

I realized that I had to go through that because I'm used to getting what I want. Then I would, I guess to some degree, harass him. But here's the thing. He never stayed away. He befriended two of my best friends who were the ones I hung out with all the time. He would hang out with us, and he was the only guy with me and my friends. There was a dynamic, and I always felt it, and he was there, and I just knew. But it was not happening for some reason. When at that moment that he ended up entertaining that gal, which I knew would end up not good, I just called it out. I was like, "These Christians are phonies." And I left.

That's when I left to Florida to serve at the church and stayed for ten months. The pastor there was so amazing. He was very transparent, but he had a heavy stronghold that led him to a downfall, and today, he is no longer on the pulpit. I pray to God that through this book we can reconnect somehow. Because believe it or not, had it not been for that season in Florida under his teaching, I would not be as bold as I am today, this transparent Christian and closer to the Lord.

I think that him no longer teaching taught me that even pastors are human, and that's important to know that they are. He was an amazing person, but he also fell, and I realize that Christians are humans. Some of them try to live in this bubble. Society, humanity, no one's perfect, and the fact that I have this tangible incident in my life that people hold onto and can refer to like, "Oh, so-and-so's daughter, she's the one that went crazy. Oh, you know what, my friend from college, she shroomed, and she had a crazy trip."

Then any time you act a little off, they relate it back to that. I let it define me for way, way too long. Someone used to tease and say, "Oh, Julio was just playing hard to get for three years because when it finally happened, it just happened." Maybe that's a gift I have—to be able to see. I'm not a fortune teller. I don't have Jesus in a crystal ball, but I guess I have discernment, and there are times I just know. I'll say this much that my husband is my most precious gift from God. He was given to me for us both to serve our purpose here. He is my greatest blessing. As a lot of people get it backward, God's hierarchy is Him, marriage, children, then work, and whatever else. If you do any of these things out of that order, your marriage will always suffer. Truth be told. #truestory.

In fact, in our marriage vows, I say that he's my gift from God to me here on earth. He is my gift, and I am his gift. What do you do with a gift? When someone gives you a gift, you cherish it. He's my gift. He's my partner. He's my yin. I'm the yang. Complete opposites but I would not be writing this book without my love, the love that drives me nuts, the love of my life after that love saga. It isn't marital bliss.

I love him. I would not be where I'm at today if I wouldn't have walked down the aisle on October 15, 2011. He is the love of my life. I married the love of my life, and it isn't marital bliss.

CHAPTER 22

Blended Family

I consciously made the decision to marry a man with two boys before our two girls. I co-parent. I have an eighteen-year-old and a sixteen-year-old son, but for some reason, people don't give you credit for your stepchildren. I guess it's because they don't know, or they assume that the relationship isn't real.

It's been a challenge, but I'm blessed to have them, the boys, because I learned early on that it was a calling to marry my husband with two boys and that I made a conscious decision to marry three men.

It's my pet peeve when people think that I don't have two sons because, mind you, yes, I can never replace their mother, but in her absence I am a Mother to them as well. A stepparent whether mother/father is a parent in the absence of their biological parent. I step in and be a parent. I am their mother figure every other week when they're at our house.

We're a blended family, and we do our best. What that means is that my husband's ex-wife and I have always had somewhat of a rare type of relationship. Pretty rare.

I remember the first day I met her at a soccer game. She came up to me and shook my hand and said *hi* very confidently. I also very confidently said *hi* back. I didn't know what to expect. However, I do know that I always would pray that we would be able to have a decent relationship. It's funny because my parents never questioned the fact that I was dating a man with two kids.

Honest, I couldn't even believe I was attracted to him, and he had two kids. It was quite odd. Although what really turned me on was the fact that he was doing the single-dad thing. He also drove this nice truck and I thought it was HOT! He looked like he had it all together until we got married, and I realized he didn't have it all together. LOL.

The whole blended family thing is hard because you're like intertwined, knowing you married this man who has an ex-wife whom also is the mother of his children. If it's a rare case, like how the ex and I get along, you'll do your best to co-parent, as we do.

However, there are some things that I can never ever fathom.

People perceive that it's not the norm that an ex-wife and the new wife would get along, but she's the one that in the beginning years of my marriage to my husband told me that they just weren't for each other, but she always prayed he would find somebody good and that she would be a good parent to the kids.

The calling to be a stepparent is one that is not for everyone. I knew what I was signing up for and since day one have treated the boys as if they were my own. It's hard because I don't feel I get recognition. The role of a stepparent is one of the most unmerited jobs.

My in-laws and my husband's ex-wife still intertwine. After all, she was married to him seven years. They're both so intertwined that there is still communication between she and my in-laws regularly. Many perceive that I am jealous over this. It's not jealousy. I just think it's weird, just because she was the one that chose to divorce. It's not the norm I think to communicate on the regular with the woman that walked out on your son and grandkids. This has actually created a strain on the relationship between my husband and his parents for some time. The hardest thing is that they're oblivious to it all. Then I feel like my in-laws assume that I'm jealous or something. I know very well that my husband is in love with me, however, I know it was devastating for him when she made the decision to divorce.

What I think people need to understand is that my husband has been true with me. I could be lying, but no, he has been true with me in that he was trying to fight for his marriage, but she didn't. Obviously, no one likes divorce; it sucks. But the reality is that she made her decision.

I think that that's devastating because you don't want to break up the family. I think my husband's family from the outside looking in make it seem like I may be jealous because at the time, most certainly he loved her, and he was in so much pain; but I happen to know the depth of the whole story. Of course it hurt to be left and rejected and not wanted anymore, and he was upset that he had to watch his kids suffer above it all. He hurt for his kids more than anything.

However, at the same time, he realizes, obviously, they weren't meant to be and thank God, right? She did me a favor after all because then we wouldn't be together. LOL.

I had a discussion one time with his ex, and she mentioned that she thought that my husband was just still angry at her and hadn't been over it. I said, "Well, no, he's frustrated about the way you parent and how difficult it is because we're night and day." My inclination was that she perceived that he was so angry, still hurting because of the divorce, which most definitely is not the case. But then, it's so much stuff, like people will perceive that. The reality is that no one has been in my shoes. It's wrong to treat the new wife as second best, and although it's not directly said, it is definitely assumed and perceived at times and does hurt. Very few women would be willing to take on the role I have had—to be no. 1, the new wife, no. 2, a mother to children she didn't bear. Neither one of these two insinuate that the former wife was no. 1, more loved or my husband's true love, no. 2, that because I didn't give childbirth to our boys that I am not just as much a mother to them as their biological mother. Again, these are all simply assumptions and perceptions of others *not mine*.

I know he had a relative that once told me, "Well, we just saw him so devastated, so I don't know if it was because she was the love of his life." Not sure how you can say that to his new wife. I get, though, people just don't know.

People seem to not understand that people move on. It's like people see in the movies or think like, "Oh, people are devastated." My husband's like, when he's done, he's done. It's been frustrating to deal with personalities and people making assumptions of you. It's hard because I know the truth.

Sometimes, it's a little difficult, especially because of our parenting, discipline styles. That's what's the worst. It seems, and it's always been perceived that we're more bad cop, and she's more good cop.

But as long as they're healthy and there's no resentment, it'll work out. The way I see it is that I can be at war with this woman or make the best of it while we're raising our children because let's face it, she'll be in my life for the rest of my life, whether I like it or not. So I'd rather make it a pleasant surprise. I mean, sorry, a pleasant experience.

Being a mother is just so incredible, especially to my two beautiful little girls. I'm fascinated by how much these two little girls adore their mama. They adore me, and they have no idea how much of a mess I am. The fact that kids just love without knowing and I constantly think if I'm doing a good job or not, I must be doing something right to earn this love, like overbearing love. They want to be with me all the time. God, if they only knew what a mess up I was.

I am filled with an outpouring of love, and that's what I needed. I needed to have these kiddos that just love me. They validate that I'm doing something right. Even in the midst of all my chaos, there is a method to my madness and my scatterbrain. I'm not anymore abnormal, less normal, or even more normal than anyone.

CHAPTER 23

Western Medicine

Call me bipolar, call me whatever. I have to tell you that I'm on meds right now. I take twenty milligrams of Fluoxetine. Fluoxetine is generic for Prozac. And I take one hundred milligrams of Lamotrigine, which is generic for Lamictal. Now we all know Prozac is an antidepressant and one of the good ones.

I'm blessed that it works for me. Lamictal is a mood stabilizer. But you can have a bad reaction to it; you can get a fatal rash that on many occasions, I've had hypochondria when I've had to start taking it because if I see any redness in the skin, I immediately think I'm getting the fatal rash. I actually have met somebody that actually got the fatal rash, which was really rare, and saw pictures. It's pretty scary.

I haven't always been on medication in the last twenty years. My exact words to Dr. Lardon in those seasons have been the following, "I don't need them. I'm fine right now. I'm not going to take them, or I'm fine."

However, ever since last year that I decided to get back on them, I embrace the fact there's a genetic disposition somewhere in my family line. I finally realized that. When you embrace that, that I'm more susceptible, it all makes sense.

Dr. Lardon would always tell me, "I know it's something. You have some type of genetic disposition because you took those mushrooms twenty years ago with seven of your buddies, and you're the only one that woke up naked and ran into the street in a blanket thinking the end of the world was coming. Your brain is wired differently." But I was nineteen at the time.

I was just like, "You're putting me on psych meds?"

He was like, "Yeah, because you fried your brains out. You go to the school on the top of the hill. All of you crazy kids partying up have no idea. You are so lucky you're right here. You are so lucky. I have kids in mental hospitals that are never coming back, never, ever coming back."

First of all, when I got out of Charter Behavioral Health, they were sending me to weird doctors who didn't listen to me when I said the medicine wasn't working.

I got released, and I was going through that weird phase that you go through. I think that you know there's a God, but then you get to the point that you're like, "Oh, I'm doing this whole life on my own."

I grew up knowing there was somebody, but I thought I was capable; in my own mind, my own strength, I could do it all. You choose where you put your faith and what you put your faith in.

That was the God that I prayed to, and he showed up at that mental hospital when on the outside looking in, I didn't know if I was coming back.

I saw this light just telling me that I would come out of this and that I would be okay. And that light, in that moment, gave me strength. I wasn't religious at the time, even though we were raised Catholic. My mom even went so far to bring Catholic ladies to anoint me with oil at our house.

She was desperate. Imagine a mother witnessing her little girl losing her mind, you know?

I remember telling my mom I'm still not okay. And that they were giving me the wrong meds. I have covered that Prozac is an antidepressant. Lamictal is a mood stabilizer. At all times, there are different meds for different things. I had been in a psychosis. There's different types of medicine to counter psychosis. There's schizophrenia; there's schizoaffective; there's bipolar, etc.

When I asked Dr. Lardon for my diagnosis, he said, "I'm not a doctor of diagnoses." He never labeled me this or that.

Never.

He did say, "You obviously had a drug-induced psychosis." I went crazy off of the drugs.

All of the chemicals in my brain were just going wild. My dopamine/serotonin levels in my brain were shot up. On the first visit to Dr. Lardon's office, he drew my brain on his dry-erase board and told me we needed to get my brain back to baseline with meds.

In my mind, I was thinking, "Meds are for crazy people. I don't need meds."

I didn't want to take them. I fought it like every other person that thinks that if they take a medication, it defines them. The reality is, what I take now, 20mg of Prozac and 100mg of Lamictal, is such a light dose. Now having to be on antipsychotic meds that is a different story. Yeah, those are the meds that everybody says turn you crazy, and suicidal. Yes, the side effects can suck. They suck. They suck. They suck.

I knew that I was not balanced at the time.

I wasn't normal, the mushrooms had done such a number on me that I fried my brain out. So I needed to get on this treatment plan to get back to baseline because I wasn't thinking rationally. And yeah, people say, "Pray about it."

Dr. Lardon treated a patient years ago, a woman who was doing well while on her medical treatment plan. She was doing somewhat okay and attending a very fundamental Christian church.

The church told her to just pray and that perhaps she didn't need the meds. So she got off her medicine. And then she started hearing voices to kill her children. The church kept telling her just to pray. She kept praying, kept praying, but inevitably in the end, she killed her children.

The church just told her to keep praying about it and that she was fine off her meds. As a result, Dr. Lardon had to testify that she was guilty by insanity. He had to pay her a visit in prison and put her back on medication. It was then she realized what she had done.

You cannot get into a person's brain. No one could have gotten into my brain at that mental hospital. You don't know what's going on in a person's brain. You don't know the spiritual battles they are battling. You don't know. So stop judging, stop perceiving, stop thinking. Look, this is the way it is. You have no idea how it is. That's the reality.

For me, people tie everything when I act crazy to this tangible incident that ended up being really gossip about me flipping out.

Today I can own up to the fact I did flip out. I could say I flipped out on drugs, and know I am more susceptible. I mentioned, although I never did mushrooms again, I did do and loved cocaine. It's like I had lived up to being a Colombiana.

I loved to play pool. I would say, "Yep, give me some of my Colombian. I'm playing eight-ball."

What I loved, I don't know, but it was drug and life abuse. It is drug abuse. I was abusing my life by using drugs. The ironic thing is that my family is from the country that is the biggest supplier of cocaine. However, Colombian people hate being defined by that. Tell us we make the best coffee in the world as well as beautiful emeralds, flowers, beautiful people, music, etc. but not COCAINE please!

I ended up spiraling down another two times. I had a horrible incident in 2000 when I tried to go back to San Diego. I wasn't exactly doing drugs, but just going back to the same environment triggered a relapse. I don't think I was trying to get off my meds. I was thinking I was okay. And then Dr. Lardon put me back on my meds. Okay, fine. I was like, "Okay. I'm fine." Even though I was thinking like freaking meds are like crazy. And then I was like, "So what am I right now?" And then, I was trying to rationalize better. Dr. Lardon was like, "Well, you probably have some bipolar tendencies." Bipolar? Doesn't that mean like a bunch of celebrities they say are bipolar?

Our brains are so very powerful. It triggered being in the same environment. It just triggered the relapse.

I had guilt. I can't remember what meds I was on in 2000 because I did a whole different cocktail of meds then.

I was suicidal at a point. I woke up one day while Dr Lardon had me on various meds experimenting which one(s) would be the perfect cocktail for my brain and I woke up in the middle of the night, and I wanted to take all these pills in my pantry. I was already downstairs in the kitchen when my mom woke up in that instance. Yes, that was all due to the side effects being so bad. But you know what? I ended up powering through those side effects because I knew I needed the medicine at that point in time.

Granted, I went back into doing cocaine, and it wasn't good.

My very last breakdown happened in 2006 when I was a successful mortgage broker services owner, living and partying it up in Los Angeles.

I did the worst thing that any person can do to a friend, a girlfriend, a best friend and tried to downplay it. I got with my best friend's ex, my best friend's boyfriend at the time, ex-boyfriend. I don't even remember what was going on. But I was so out there, on a high because I was making money. I was living in Los Angeles.

I don't even have to tell you that specific story, but the reason I ended up getting with him is because we were suite mates in the same business building on Wilshire Blvd.

There I came, just starting up my company from my home office in Corona, and he wasn't making enough money to pretty much pay the rent on Wilshire Blvd. So I moved to Los Angeles to sublease with him and never looked back.

It was one of the best times of my life until I lost everything. I asked my parents to take out an equity line on their house of $250,000 to invest in my business. I literally thought I was going to be the next Latina Trump. I had a friend that used to tell me that I had a drive for business and a drive to help people.

I don't see money as an object. I see money as a means of survival. I don't feel like I need to hold on to it. I feel like you move it. You move it here; you move it there. And you lose it too.

I got back on meds last year. I had been off of them for about a couple of years, but I always got postpartum, and then I didn't, and then I got on them, then I got off. But when the stress happens, I just need them. I don't know. And it's not because I'm weaker or I'm not praying about it. No, God told me. I prayed in that mental hospital. And he sent me Dr. Michael Lardon that today because of him I was led to share my story. Dr Lardon is a psychiatrist in the mainstream now, very well known, treating elite athletes.

How is that possible? The God I prayed to sent me a man with so much wisdom on how to exactly treat me. It's the abuse of medication that is bad. I don't care what you do. Pray about it. Get a pastoral counselor. You seek the Holy Spirit; you seek the Lord. God is my great physician, and I did pray to Him, but He didn't just miraculously heal me. He sent me a medical doctor. So sometimes medication is needed. And I am grateful for medical intervention.

You guys think that you could say, "Oh, well, just do this. Do exercise." I told that to Dr. Lardon so many times, and his answer was like, "Fine. Go ahead. Go exercise. But every two to three years, life happens. Stress. You're not going to always eat good. You're not going to always be perfect. You're not. That's the reality, and you have this ability. You're more susceptible than most people, and you already have something."

And people think that when he tells me that, that it's a lie or something. That I should, "Oh, no, no, no, you're believing that? Just overcome that. It's just because you don't watch your life." No, everybody's wired differently, and if I choose to stay on medication off and on for the rest of my life, so what? I'm on it. I've been on it for a year now. I don't know. Don't ask me if I'm going to get off of it. I don't know, and I don't care. I may or may not. I don't care. So what if I stayed on it? I have to pop these pills until the day I die. So what? My grandmother used to pop a freaking storage Ziploc bag, gallon bag of seventeen medications. She lived to be eighty-seven, but she took that medication with faith. That's what it is.

You're giving false advice, and I don't know where you're getting it from. That's why a medical doctor is backing me up. Some people need it; some people don't. What works for everybody won't work for you.

Break these stigmas. Stop judging people. Okay? That kid in Florida that shot up the school, it wasn't him; it was his mind. The gun doesn't kill by itself. Our pastor shared in a message on a Sunday, the following, "You know what? Take away the gun. They'll throw rocks." So stop it. Stop, stop, stop. Stop judging. Stop it now. All right?

It's the human mind. It's a matter of the heart. Heart and mind needs to connect. A knife doesn't kill or stab by itself. It's the person, the human being behind it. It's the fact that that kid went untreated. Maybe his parents were ashamed because there is shame in admitting anxiety and depression. There's shame in admitting we have a family member that's crazy. They're ashamed until that family member is out on the street, homeless, going crazy. They're ashamed. Where does that shame get you? Who cares? Get out there, and get better, and help people get better. Stop putting them in a box.

CHAPTER 24

Driving under the Influence

On December 2, 2017, I got a DUI at thirty-nine years old. Never in my life had I gotten a DUI. I mean, come on, everyone drives with a little buzz.

I was at an ugly sweater party with some girlfriends, drinking some red wine and having a great time. I had been on this little wine kick, and I thought I was just fine to drive home.

It was around the holidays, and I had been attending many networking events for work. So I actually had been Ubering around that time too, which was pretty odd, but interestingly enough, I drove home. I was pretty close to home, and since I was buzzed, naturally I wanted bad food. I went through a fast food drive-through, got myself a burger with fries and a Dr. Pepper.

Then after, I turned onto the cross street near my home. What happened next was that I got into an accident, and I hit a parked car because I was bending down to get my food.

That night and that moment, it was the point of my return *for reals*! God testing his stubborn, dumb sheep thinking she is in control. I honestly thought I would get away by leaving a note. But God I think was like, "Nope! I am going to test you one more time so you can learn to *slow your roll* one last time." People, learn from me. Don't learn things the hard way. The neighbors came out and called the cops on me. I had no idea they did either. I was getting ready to drive off after exchanging all my information with the neighbors. And just as I was getting in the car, the cops pulled up.

I didn't deny the test. I really didn't know much about DUIs.

But everything came back like a flashback of being cuffed and taken in 5150. But this time, I wasn't tripping on drugs but to a degree impaired due to the wine.

When I got booked and put in that cell for the longest eight to twelve hours of my life, I was utterly in tears. I couldn't believe that here I went again. "Why me, God? I'm not even a drunk." I was having high anxiety and probably on the verge of a nervous breakdown in that jail cell for the night. Thank God, for my God sent hubby whom I was able to call from the pay phone in the cell because his number was a local number. My husband actually laughed at me. He wasn't even mad. He was more like, "I told you that you were getting carried away again." How humiliating too, right? After all, I am Christian. You know that as a Christian, you're supposed to be perfect. Not!

However though, God spoke to me this time hard. I'm not a nineteen-year-old kid just tripping on drugs. Now I'm a wife and mama. It was a huge eye opener and reality check.

When I shared with Dr. Lardon about the DUI at an office visit with my hubby, he chuckled and shared with my husband, "That is a shame. I have never known your wife to be a drunk."

The aftermath of a DUI—costs, attorney fees, license suspension, restricted license, SR22 insurance binder, and the most lovely of them all is DUI education aka four months of inconvenient and boring classes where the reality of alcoholism and drunk driving is explicitly being thrown at you like no other. Thankful that my DUI education instructor is the sweetest and wisest eighty-nine-year-old, thirty-nine years sober, ex-alcoholic.

A good friend who had gone through this all in the previous year told me the following:

"Don't replay what happened that night over and over. You could have, but you didn't, just deal with it all and do what needs to be done. It's too late!"

And that is exactly what I have done.

The twist, though, is that again, *everything does really happen for a reason.*

CHAPTER 25

Concluding Interview

Attorney Patrick Silva is my DUI attorney, which is why I share the live interviews with him throughout my book. The main reason being, he was floored the day he met me for the first time in his office. He was amazed about how open and vulnerable I was about sharing everything in regards to going 5150. The one thing I asked and was very concerned about was that I wanted to know what shows up on my DMV record. He naturally asked why, I mentioned that back in college, I had gone 5150 due to a shroom trip. "I'm not crazy, though. I was on drugs."

He looked at me and laughed with so much amazement about how open I was. He asked, "Why don't you share about this more? I can't believe you're so open about going 5150." At that point, I mentioned I was writing a book and that the doctor that treated me for twenty years was writing my foreword.

I mentioned that I had been having writer's block. So I was at a standstill in the book-authoring process. I proceeded to let him know that it was hard to put the traumatic parts of my story into words. He then mentioned, "Why don't you dictate your story?"

He had written a book on DUIs in that same matter.

He said, "The way you're so authentic and transparent about it all, you need to share." And so there you have it. Had it not been for the DUI and me meeting Patrick Silva, this book would not have come to fruition. I dictated over thirty-seven voice memos that were transcribed.

A gal I hired had to go through all those voice memos/transcriptions and give some order to this book. This book is unique in format, just as its author. I invite you to read along and witness the last interview/conclusion of my story.

PATRICK SILVA: Hello, this is attorney Patrick Silva with Aileen Mezza today, and we'll be discussing the mental-health rights of people. Primarily, when do people treat other people like dirt? Aileen was in a mental hospital, and we're going to talk a little bit about how she felt about this. Can you hear me okay?

AILEEN MEZZA. Yes.

PATRICK SILVA. All right. I want you to take a deep breath and kind of tell me, going back to that point in time. Close your eyes and talk to me about it, putting yourself in the point where you were reading stuff on the walls.

AILEEN MEZZA. I've had three major breakdowns in my life. In those three episodes, I was probably hospitalized in one, two, three, four, five different mental hospitals. The first time, nothing, I was too far out to have read anything because I was on the shrooms. Yeah, I was too far out. The first time was really bad. The second time, I actually went back to San Diego, and something in my mind triggered like a relapse. I wasn't even on drugs.

I got taken to Sharp Institute in San Diego, a mental hospital. I don't know if it's still there. My doctor had told me that it's no longer there. I can vividly remember that time. My girlfriends thought I wasn't okay due to high anxiety, so they called my parents. They came from Orange County to get me in San Diego. By the time they arrived, I was actually doing and feeling a lot better. It was when they came for me to take me back home that I actually went into convulsions back at our house in Buena Park, California. I don't know, like I was demon possessed or something. It was really odd, I went 5150, my doctor had me admitted over to Sharp. When I got to Sharp, and was walking the hallways of the ward, oddly enough, I was intrigued because there was something on the wall that read the rights of mental patients.

Mind you, I was there for a breakdown, a mental patient. I actually was reading because I am compelled to read stuff like that, and as I read it, I was asking myself in my head, "Okay, I have rights in here?" Then in that moment right when I was still reading, I don't even think I finished reading it, is when the nurse on duty on the ward that night looked at what I was reading, and I think she was trying to get my attention to either go take my medicine, I can't even remember, or get in the room.

I said, "I'm reading this." I said, "Why are you being so mean?" Like, "Let me finish." She's like, "No, go to your room." I was like, "Yeah, you're a human being just like me. I'm reading. Don't I have rights in here?" Like, "Why are you treating me like this?" Like, "You're a human being just like me."

PATRICK SILVA. Let me ask you this question. Might boggle you. I want you to change places with that nurse. I want you to be her right now. She sees you reading on the wall. What's going through her mind?

AILEEN MEZZA. Honestly—

PATRICK SILVA. Why is she frustrated? Why did she treat you that way? I think that's kind of the crux—why did this human treat another human with such disdain and disrespect? What is going on in her mind? Let's not make excuses, but let's explore.

AILEEN MEZZA. My honest, honest opinion is that the people that work in those clinics, mental hospitals are extremely frustrated.

PATRICK SILVA. What about her? Was she frustrated?

AILEEN MEZZA. I couldn't say, but you're dealing with mental patients all day. You don't know which ones are what level, what patients are at another level, you can't get in their brains. You just know they're all mental patients. I'm sure there's a frustration that comes with being in her position.

PATRICK SILVA. When does her frustration justify her?

AILEEN MEZZA. She's in authority.

PATRICK SILVA. She's your god.

AILEEN MEZZA. As a mental patient, you have no credibility whatsoever, even if she was in the wrong. Sadly, she then used her authority, proceeded and injected me with who knows what to sedate me. The last thing I remember was her throwing me into the asylum where all I saw was white walls. I was crying and couldn't believe a human being that was in a position to care for me could actually use her control that way. I was so scared. Again, I prayed and must have knocked out and woken up. In regards to her, what I would say is that her frustration led her to just want to put out the fire. In conversation with my close friends in the psych field they have shared that they have witnessed when having to do rounds at a psych clinic that it is very true in fact that the nurses do get very frustrated.

PATRICK SILVA. It's an easy way out?

AILEEN MEZZA. Exactly, pretty much. The fact is I don't know. The hospital later ended up being shut down I was told. It was closed for not meeting proper codes. I'm sure something funky must have been going on. The last thing I could remember was us arguing, then she was so frustrated that I was questioning her that it is when she proceeded to inject me with who knows what, and she threw me in a room with white walls, everything was spinning, she had drugged me up so much. And I remember just being like, "Oh my gosh. Is this really happening? I feel even crazier now." That's where the problem lies, these institutions just make you crazier, it's like you're one big human experiment. I was not an animal. I was a human being just like the nurse who injected me. But this is the study of the brain, you can't get into someone's head. Nevertheless, it's a trauma that I had to live through. It is something I have stored away for years, but today am finally bringing to the light. I don't want others to have to continue to suffer what I had to endure under supposedly psych care. And all I want is true justice and TRUE MENTAL HEALTH RIGHTS.

Perhaps professionals in the field of psychology need to go through more training and screening to before put on assignment to begin treating mental patients. I don't know. Now in retrospect, I met you through my DUI, and I just told you earlier when I got here the coincidental thing about this all is that I went to jail through this whole ordeal, on December 2,

157

2017, and I wondered why this all happened. Now I have two perspectives. I was an inmate, and I've been a mental patient. I really don't know what's worse, I guess they treat you like crap in both places, right? I think the difference is when you're in jail, you have a reason to be there. Most of the time, they have a reason to arrest you. The 5150 is you're a danger to yourself or to society. How can they prove that? How could they prove that I was really a danger to myself or to society? Because of false perception. That's what my book's about, *Look, This Is the Way It Is: A Perspective of Life through the Lenses of a Very Real Chick*. It's the perception they have of mental patients. It's the perception because you can't get into a person's brain. You can't.

PATRICK SILVA. Let's go with that. So the perception that a person has of another person, right?

AILEEN MEZZA. Yes.

PATRICK SILVA. Can we go…let's go back to the most basic perception. Color of skin, right? Let's go back one hundred years. You don't know the person, but you can make a judgment based on what you see of their skin, what you think?

AILEEN MEZZA. Right.

PATRICK SILVA. Right? Here we are one hundred years later. They're making a perception based on what they've been taught about. Basically, if I'm hearing you right, they've been biased against you through their education.

AILEEN MEZZA. Pretty much.

PATRICK SILVA. Now they're at a level of authority over you where no matter how wrong or how badly they treat you, it's okay.

AILEEN MEZZA. Right. The only person that could speak for you is probably, at that point, your medical doctor, but I wasn't even able to tell my medical doctor until like years later because I even feel like had I told him at that moment, I was still his patient. Would he have believed me then?

PATRICK SILVA. Because so many tell him that. They all tell him that.

AILEEN MEZZA. Exactly. The fact of the matter was when… I can't even remember when I told him. I might have told him five years ago, and that happened in 2000. I specifically remember Dr. Michael Lardon saying…"Why didn't you ever tell me that that happened?" It's like, "Well, I was the mental patient. Would you have even believed me?"

A diagnosis can never define me because I won't let it. The reality is I had a drug-induced psychosis my first episode, in 1998. Now when I'm on drugs, when I'm acting crazy, I'm acting bipolar, but when I'm not that, then it's my normal, right? I'm being normal, so I don't care what people call me. They can call me manic. They can call me bipolar. I know I'm not. I know. I think the sad thing is definitely that more awareness needs to be spread about mental health.

When I first spoke with my literary agent at my publisher, she immediately said, "Wow. What better time for you now to release this book." I feel it because it's everywhere, and people… I was blessed to have great resources. I found this amazing doctor who's writing my foreword and amen. There's a lot of people that don't know what to do. There's not enough education. People are stigmatized, so they don't want to go get the help. People want to just like, "Oh, I'll do it naturally. I'll pray about it."

PATRICK SILVA. Let me ask you this then. Do you think society is overmedicated? Because when I turn on the TV, I try not to watch it. It goes back to me as a kid where we got one hour of TV a day. That was it. My mom would feel the TV when she came home, right? To tell if it was on.

AILEEN MEZZA. Really?

PATRICK SILVA. Oh yeah. All right, but if you watch, do you think there's an overprescription of drugs? I'm just trying to, wondering, do you think drugs could have led to part of your problem?

AILEEN MEZZA. The drug-induced psychosis was definitely the shrooms. That was what… I don't know if I had said that in my first recording. Definitely the shrooms did a thing on me, but there was definitely some genetic disposition. Because on my dad's side of the family, we are genetically disposed.

PATRICK SILVA. Okay, all right.

AILEEN MEZZA. That's why my doctor says because the day that I shroomed, I shroomed with seven of my friends, and I'm the only one that walked on Montezuma Road in a blanket naked, thinking the end of the world was coming. I told my doctor that I have some genetic disposition. I did ask my psychologist, actually my very first psychologist who's now retired. I spoke with him last week for twenty minutes. He's in Seattle. I asked if it would have come out had I not done drugs. He couldn't answer that.

PATRICK SILVA. Damn.

AILEEN MEZZA. He couldn't answer that.

PATRICK SILVA. What if we're two hundred years ago and you're with the tribal elder who's shrooming, right?

AILEEN MEZZA. Mmhmm (affirmative).

PATRICK SILVA. You're seeing these things where now you're a talisman. Two hundred years ago, that trip that you went down, that would have been, you would have been the leader of the tribe. You would have been the spiritual leader.

AILEEN MEZZA. There you go.

PATRICK SILVA. Right.

AILEEN MEZZA. Spiritual because my faith is a big part of this. I have always wanted to be open and share my story. However, the only reason I finally did is because Dr. Lardon agreed to validate it by writing the forward of my book. And not only that but the fact that his MD will be on the cover is huge for me. It gives me credibility that I feel I can never have earned otherwise because I have been so busy going and going all these years, looking to heal from all this trauma. Sure I made poor decisions that led me to the places I ended up at. But was the mistreatment necessary. Maybe God did allow it all for a reason? I needed Dr Lardon to a degree to vouch for me that I'm not crazy. And after all, it's a world of titles, right?

PATRICK SILVA. Mmhmm (affirmative).

AILEEN MEZZA. It's going to say, "Authored by Aileen Amador Mezza and foreword by Dr. Michael Lardon, MD" because I'm afraid, yeah, to be like, there's that part of me that says society's going to be like, "Well, she's just someone that went crazy." Right?

PATRICK SILVA. That's okay. What's wrong with that?

AILEEN MEZZA. Because the reality is everyone's a little crazy.

PATRICK SILVA. Yeah. What's wrong with you just being crazy and writing the dang book?

AILEEN MEZZA. That's what I did.

PATRICK SILVA. Yeah.

AILEEN MEZZA. "I wanted to share with you whom I dedicated the book to. A year ago when I started on this writing project, I didn't know who to dedicate it to because I was like, 'Who do you dedicate a book to anyway?'" LOL. Then last week, as I was approaching my final recordings, God confirmed it. Ironically, I have a deceased bestie, that at twenty-two years old, was killed by a drunk driver in broad daylight in Orange County.

PATRICK SILVA. Wow.

AILEEN MEZZA. Karina was one of a kind, she went to San Diego with me. She was a ray of light. Her sister actually at the time had written a book. Karina loved San Diego just as much as I did I believe, we escaped to college to get away from our home life and problems, that's for sure. I fondly remember her always referring to San Diego and always wanting to say the following: "San Diego, baby." My dedication was, "To this crazy world we call home for now." Then I did a two-part dedication, "To my gorgeous friend, K.I.D., Karina Irma Davidds, who left this world way too soon, and rest in our eternal home until we meet again." Then I put, "San Diego, baby." And then also the second part dedication is "To this crazy world we all call home." And the truth is everyone's a little crazy.

PATRICK SILVA. Yeah.

CHAPTER 26

The Way It Is

Everybody has their own treatment plans, and I think I've said that you can pray, go and seek a pastoral counselor, go seek a holistic doctor. Do whatever, but everyone's unique. You can't be put in a box because you went to church, and they're just telling you to pray about your anxiety, your depression, your highs and your lows.

No, you pray. You pray first. #Godfirst.

You pray, and you seek help.

You find that peace, the inner peace, whatever way.

I pray, and I don't mean whatever way is possible because my faith lies on Jesus Christ. That's who I believe in. He needs to come in and touch your life. You need to want to get better.

You need to want to change, so you need to seek Him and pray.

One of my pet peeves is thinking that Christianity is also a religion. It's not. What's the word in Christian? It's Christ. I choose to put my faith in Christ.

He is my rock.

Honestly, I don't just say the following to make myself feel better. But I believe everyone has their acute battles with mental illness. And you know what? That is *okay*!

Life happens! Thank God, we have God to rest on. Amen!

It dawned on me that I've allowed this perception of the eyes that people have had on me or the thoughts because I'm not just someone that just observes visibly; I observe auditorily and kinetically. Nicholoas Fitante, MFT, pointed this out to me when he was letting me know how everyone is different and that what may work for one person may not work for another.

All those three men in this field the PhD, the MD, and the MFT have been such a blessing to me. Helping me understand it all better so that I am able to cope with it all better. Knowledge is key.

I have to honestly say that without them all and their push, this book would not have become a reality.

The one thing I lament in my life is that I'm barely about to enter my senior year of college online. After twenty years of going in but really, it is never too late. I actually didn't want to write this book until I myself had a PhD, MD, or MFT.

I've always feared that if I didn't have those credentials, the world would just recognize me and perceive me the same way most of my inner sphere has always done, no one but myself knows the pain it caused me to live and force to overcome. Thank you to my professional psych care, my doctors and therapists, the people that have seen and validated me for who I am, have seen my struggles, and know the Aileen of today—they again have given me all the credibility I needed to share my story.

I'm no psychologist; I'm not.

But I learned from the best, the best life coaches. I am grateful for the field of psychology, and so with that being said, I wrote this book so people would seek resources, the proper ones.

I'm not knocking anyone. I was just that person that tried it all, and I'm grateful. I know that I would not be sane today had there not been medical intervention. It's crazy because I feel like I am; if you looked at my credit report, which shows all the student loans I have out, one would think I should probably be a doctor by now.

I believe, and I've always believed people have come to me for advice. I give the best device. I really do. I just never take it. I think that's human nature too. So I think I've been that friend to everybody. I guess I have wise things to say, but it's only because I've learned from the best.

You meet people from twenty years ago or something. Maybe you had a falling out. Maybe you didn't, or you haven't seen each other, but that's when you know you're friends. You just pick up from where you left off, as if there was no absence in time and space.

There's no order in anything I do. On those days that I'm feeling extra, extra crazy, I can call myself crazy, extra all over the place because I thrive off of being on the go.

I thrive on being everywhere, and I'm always running late. I always have some excuse, but it's really not an excuse. It's really what happened. I know that I have to get better at that, like getting my daughter to school on time. I have to respect people's time, but because I'm always on the go and on those days, I feel like I can't help it. I'm not perfect, and I will never pretend to be.

This process has been so liberating. I am so grateful to the Lord that I have been able to get my story out. Thank you, God, for allowing me to live the life You designated for me to live.

I look forward to what's to come.

#mentalhealth #falseperceptions #Godfirst #breakingstigmas

*A*nd this *CAME...*

My intention was never to add this insert to my book. But inevitably, LIFE HAPPENED, once again.

The final words in my last chapter ended with:

"I look forward to what it is to come…"

Let me begin by sharing that my publishing process took a pause due to a life changing event that occurred on August 19th, 2018.

So…

What was that life changing event?

"The CT scan revealed that you have a mass on the right side of your (my husband's) brain. We must admit you right away."

These were the words that were said to us in that quiet room in ER on Sunday, Aug 19th, 2018.

I will never forget that moment for as long as I live; it is forever embedded in my mind.

> Alone, together, in that room, in silence.
> Julio (my husband): It's going to be okay
> Aileen: Yes, GOD's got this!! We're going to
>   power through…

And the very next thing we did in that quiet room was close our eyes and pray together.

Some might wonder if we were afraid in those moments following the doctor's words. If you were to ask my husband, he would say no. He said he knew that GOD would see us through everything from the moment that we heard the words about the mass on the right side of his brain. If he had feared anything, he said it would be how I would react, being that I'm normally a nervous wreck.

> "Be anxious for nothing, but in everything
> by prayer and supplication, with thanks-
> giving, let your requests be made known
> to God; and the peace of God, which sur-
> passes all understanding, will guard your
> hearts and minds through Christ Jesus."
> (Philippians 4: 6–7)

This verse has been what I've been living my entire life by. My husband has this very verse tattooed on his arm with two hands in prayer. This verse couldn't have come more alive that day in that room. **"THE PEACE OF GOD which surpasses all understanding"**. In the midst of being told this horrible news, there was this feeling of peace; That peace, is the peace that surpasses all understanding. It's the peace that comes when you have full trust in The Almighty to carry you through everything and anything.

And it was HIS peace that sustained us the first three weeks and a half of this journey. Julio & I didn't have it in ourselves alone to endure what we were to face in the coming months.

On January 27, 2019, I sat down to reflect on the months that had passed. Julio and I took our family on a little staycation away for the weekend because Julio's chemotherapy/radiation treatment was scheduled for February 5, 2019.

I wanted to sit, reflect, and finally take a moment to complete this book.

The staycation trip was not just completely for leisure. The plan was to finish my final copy edit of my book to submit to my publisher by the end of the coming week.

Let me reiterate that this is an addition to my book.

Disclaimer: If you didn't already think that my whole book, *LOOK!*, was your forte because of the lack of organization and my writing style, please don't expect this insert to be any better. In fact, expect it to be worse when it comes to being a traditional book.

I am an emotional mess more than ever these days.

Even though, I am extraordinarily grateful for so much.

First, I am grateful for GOD. Without him, I know I would not be here today. I am also grateful to Dr. Lardon (psychiatrist), Prozac (antidepressant med), Lamictal (mood stabilizer med), psychotherapists (Nicholas Fitante, Theresa, and Scott, MFTs @ ACT Family Counseling-Ontario, CA), family, good friends, church, and work.[1]

The reason I have to disclaim all of the following again is because is some ways I very well think I jinxed myself by writing "LOOK!"

As common sayings go:

"Be careful what you wish for"—Unknown

"Practice what you preach."—Unknown

"If you're going to talk the talk, you better walk the talk."—Unknown

Life is a roller coaster and can change within the blink of an eye. Julio's brain cancer ended up coming back. In December of 2019 symptoms that the brain tumor was growing again surfaced. He had his fourth and last surgery in February of 2020. As a result, he was left partially paralyzed, Coincidently, when the world was shutting down to protect people from COVID-19. At the time we had sought out every viable option for him and his treatment. We traveled, we advocated for him, we listened to many professionals go over their plan of action for him. After seeking all we could for him, he was put into hospice care in the summer of 2020. He outlived the average statistic of thirteen months, for his type of rare brain cancer, Gliosarcoma, he lived twenty-six months. He was dedicated at whatever cost to fight for his life. His biggest "why" was the love for his family. As I look back on all he endured and we endured as a family, in the end, we had to accept it was his time. Life can change in any instant. What we need to be grateful for and matters is what love was shared, what mountains we moved, and what we do after our loved one leaves us. In hindsight, I thought what I had survived in college was the hard-

---

[1] ALL exactly in the above mentioned order of priority.

est obstacle I would ever face. However, I couldn't have been more wrong. I thought I was crazy, but life is what is crazy. And I wouldn't change one thing about the life I have lived. All I ever wanted from life was to love and be loved by someone who saw the real me. Julio took his last breath on November 5, 2020, and entered into eternity. As I reflect on this all today, thankful that he left me better to know him, and love him through all the days, good and bad. He left me our two beautiful daughters and my two bonus sons. He left his mark on my heart and changed me for the better. He departed from this world, but yet I never feel alone because he resides in my heart. The memories we shared I will cherish for a lifetime. I miss him dearly and always will. God taught me, along with Julio, that with the right tools, the right people, and the right focus, my story is not over. Today I live my life focused, always looking at the light, embracing my losses, and my faults to keep me moving forward.

This insert is not intended to be very long; I just wanted to share some of the challenges that life has presented since the beginning of the writing of this book, as well as let you know about the book that's to follow. **_Faulty Me_** will document our journey from the moment Julio was diagnosed and how our faith and God's plan strengthened us. So without further ado, please enjoy the first couple of pages of my new book.

FAULTY ME

EXCERPT FROM CHAPTER I
Real Talk with Julio & Aileen

Alone, together, in that room, in silence.
Julio: **It's going to be okay**
Aileen: **Yes, GOD's got this!!**
We're going to power through…

Sometimes, life hands you challenges that leave you a little shaken. On August 19th, 2018, my husband, Julio, was told that he had a large mass on the right side of his brain. The following is our documentation of that journey.

> "My husband is scheduled for a *third* brain surgery on Thursday, December 20, 2018. On an MRI scan, inflammation and tumor growth can look similar.
>
> Unfortunately, the only way to confirm is to operate again. We met with both of his neuro-oncologists yesterday. We were leary about a third surgery. But we made this educated decision together.
>
> We will be speaking with his neurosurgeon (Dr. Lars Anker) next week. Because of the size and rapid growth, we can't just chance to wait it out to see if it's just inflammation. If it is a tumor again, then of course it needs to be taken out.

This is the last bit of news we wanted, especially, right before Christmas. Please pray. We won't lose hope. Praying it will only be inflammation."

—Aileen Mezza, December 18, 2018

Julio and I initially made the decision to seek alternative treatment.

A door opened for a clinical trial, immunotherapy, with Dr Kesari out of St John's in Santa Monica, CA. Julio and I were so blessed to have the opportunity to postpone chemo/radiation and to possibly not have to do it at all if it was not necessary. In October 2018, this is the bit of news we wanted, especially, Julio began the immunotherapy trial.

In early December after his routine MRI we were informed there was something visible and that the doctors were being proactive and not wanting to take chances with what they saw on the MRI. They were worried that what they saw was not inflammation and could be tumor regrowth. The immunotherapy trial was, unfortunately, not working for Julio. We are in the best hands and are so blessed by our amazing team of doctors at St Jude Medical Center in Fullerton, CA

They operated and they were correct. It was not inflammation and Julio's tumor had regrown. It was a true nightmare merely days before Christmas.

I asked God why this was happening when Julio had been feeling so good lately. But I put my faith in God's plan and kept reminding myself that His ways are higher; only He knows the beginning and the end of this journey.

I cry, laugh, and scream daily; but I must keep moving. I am the love of my life's full-time caregiver/wife, as well as a full-time Mama, and a full-time real estate and mortgage professional. There is no time in my schedule to sulk, although I do, because I wouldn't be human if I didn't...

PRAYER

Even when I was deep in my sadness, you were there with me. Thank you, thank you for coming to rescue me. When my life got so dark that the thought of any light was so far, thank you. Thank you, thank you that I got to share my life with the world and give you the glory. I didn't have it in myself to get out those mental places, those mental states of mind. I'm glad I sought and prayed, and I found. I sought you with all my heart and found You. Amen.

> For I know the thoughts that I think toward you, says the LORD, thoughts of peace and not of evil, to give you a future and a hope. Then you will call upon Me and go and pray to Me, and I will listen to you. And you will seek Me and find *Me,* when you search for Me with all your heart. I will be found by you, says the LORD, and I will bring you back from your captivity; I will gather you from all the nations and from all the places where I have driven you, says the LORD, and I will bring you to the place from which I cause you to be carried away captive. (Jeremiah 29:11–14, NKJV)

ACKNOWLEDGMENTS

I have come to realize something. My life is a mosaic of all the beautiful very long list if I named everyone I have crossed paths with that touched my heart, either for good and/or bad. You could learn from the ones that also bruised, hurt your heart. Those hearts still touched.

I don't need to name a list of those people. You all know who you are.

People do come into your life for a season, a reason, and a lifetime, but eventually if you're able to find that balance in life to function at your normal in this crazy world in the bigger picture and sphere of things, everything will always come full circle (360 degrees).

And that sums up the reason for the *looking* eyes on the cover of the book. It's the way you learn to perceive things and take everything for face value. I have always been a deep and intense individual, and that will remain.

So in retrospect, perhaps on the outside looking in, I can see why I have always been perceived a certain way by others. Today I just realize it's knowing when and where that deep intensity gets the best of me and my emotions. I get it all now. Look! This, that is the way it is, has been, is, will be, and will always be, if only we would accept that it is necessary to let things go and not let whatever we've allowed to define us for so long be and find freedom in the fact that we have absolutely no control over that thing, especially if it's long past. But we do have the choice on how we continue to let it affect us. You have to let things just roll off of you like butter.

Be an observer, be a lover, be a doer, have intense passion, but know your balance. Only then, you can come to the realization there is no need to knock so hard, pound so hard, try forcing doors to open that for some reason were shut in the interim of things or worst yet, forever.

But in due season, if you just wait, be patient, and when you ask wholeheartedly one random day, you'll see. *Doors do open* on their own, and you will walk in gracefully dancing or better yet singing the lyrics to Diana Ross' hit song that goes a little something like this… "I'm coming out. I want the world to know, got to let it show." And you will realize it's better that way than to run through life slumming it. YOLO (You Only Live Once).

So live your best life *now*!

Amen.

"Enter by the narrow gate; for wide is the gate and broad is the way that leads to destruction, and there are many who go in by it. Because narrow is the gate and difficult is the way which leads to life, and there are few who find it" (Matthew 7:13–14).

"Let your light so shine before men, that they may see your good works, and glorify your Father which is in heaven" (Matthew 5:16).

SPECIAL THANK YOU

Thank you Mom, Dad, & Sis for your unconditional love for this daughter and sister of yours.
Without your support I would be nothing.

I LOVE YOU

Thank you to my editor, Jenessa Mercer. God knew when we met what HE was orchestrating.
Infinitely, grateful to you my dear.
ONLY YOU can put my scatter brain thoughts into an eloquent words. LUV YA!

Thank you to my kids who are my WHY.

TO: ALL OF YOU

My bonus son's Angelo & Ian Mezza and my beautiful daughter's Zoe & Daniela Mezza
PS: You too @ Ariana Noguera, my beloved and beautiful daughter-in- law/love to be one day.
LOVE YOU SO SOO MUCH
XOXO

THANK YOU TO THE GOD OF THE UNIVERSE FOR THIS
LIFE HE DESIGNATED FOR ME TO LIVE.

Although, on this journey has tested me far greater from what I
would have ever imagined.

In the storms of LIFE I have never stopped seeing You.

Amen.

THANK YOU FOR "JULIO MEZZA" GOD

Thank you for the opportunity of being his bride, blessed beyond
measure, that You chose US for one another.

The memories we shared will last in my heart for a lifetime.

I STILL SEE YOU

*The poem below was written by the author and
shared at her late husband's memorial service,*

God, I still see You

I have seen your loving hands caryy us through this journey since day one

I saw You in that ER room on August 19th, 2018 when we were told the news of my husband's brain tumor.

I saw you there in the strength You gave my husband to accept the news and bring immediate comfort to me with the words only he could say in his most chillest demeanor,

"We're goinf to be okay"

In the midst of the fear "I Still Saw You"

I saw you in the hands of my husband's magnificent doctors and oncology staff that You blessed us with.

And in my pain and grief I still see You.

I saw You all the times I took him to ER visits and doctor visits.

I saw You carrying us and giving us hope. You were with me in the waiting room during his four brain surgeries. You have been with our children. Carrying the boys and our little girls.

God, I still see You.

I have seen Your provision and Your love. You have given us the peace that surpasses all understanding that I am aware can only come from You.

I see You in the supernatural strength You have given both my husband and I. As well as the wisdom You blessed him with that in turn he has poured unto me.

I have seen You orchestrate this beautiful love story since day one of me meeting my beloved.
I still see You.
I see how you manifested all.
I see and know wihtout a doubt You chose us for one another.
Your always are higher.
I won't question them.
The pain and grief is immense,
but I still see You.
I see You in my business affairs. I see You providing abundantly for our family despite the circumstances.
I see You in the clients I am blessed wto help and serve.
The clients that have walked this journey alongside me. Oh how You bless thee.
I still see You.
I see You every morning when I cry.
I see You in the care and help you sent.
I see You in family and friends.
I still see You.
I have seen You in the peace Yu gave us at the beginning of hospice care and the fear of the unknown.
I saw you as I lay next to my husband every night to tell him I loved him and cry with him.
God, I still see You.
I see You God becaise I know You are faithful. You have been faithful in every season. In every high and low of my past, my present, and I don't doubt You wil continue to be in the future that lies ahead.
I still see You God.
I see that taking my beloved home earlier than I would have ever imagined was part of Your sovereign will from the start.
I see You as You guide me to be the Mama bear to my little girls and our boys in the midst of the chaos and pain.
You are with me and I still see You.
When I don't have the words to console them, You intervene and send me the perfect words.
Thank You. Thank You.

I still see You God.
I will continue to see You as I awake.
I will see my beloved in our children for all the days of my life
His legacy we will carry
He lives in each of us and our hearts are fuller knowing he resides there.
I will seee him every sunrise, sunset, or just under the clear sky or under the night sky and stars
I still see You God.
The time came. You came for my beloved.
I have cried many nights.
And I will cry even more days and nights for years to come.
But one thing I know is this—
I still see You.
You are with me.
I still see You God.
Amen.

ABOUT THE AUTHOR
2019 EDITION

Aileen Amador Mezza is a woman with immense passion for life. She owes all she is to God. She is a lover of people who longs to help people find their *why* in this life, realizing that life happens. But that is *okay*. Through her life experiences and struggles to find her balance in this crazy world, she acknowledges that optimum mental health is the key to it all. She is open, transparent, and very real about what she has gone through and overcome. She studies human development at Hope International University in Fullerton, California. However, she owes a lot of the knowledge she has gained in regard to mental health throughout the last twenty years to the field of psychology. Number one, again to God and to her godsent doctor and friend Dr. Michael Lardon. Dr. Lardon specializes in sports-medicine psychiatry. He has been given the wisdom to treat many elite athletes from NFL, PGA, and Olympic athletes in the mainstream. He has written the fore-word to *LOOK! This is the way it is*. She refers to Dr. Lardon as more of a life coach in the last twenty years. He has mastered the art of helping athletes find their zone to peak perform in sports as he states in his book *Finding Your Zone*. She believes Dr. Lardon as well has been a key component to why she also with his help, helped her find her zone to peak perform in this life. Dr. Lardon had always been a fan of her sharing her story for the world to hear. Dr. Lardon gave her all the credibility she needed to share her story so she can seek to help others by giving them the vision she was given to get better with her faith and the resources the field of psychology has to offer those willing to seek the help without shame or being falsely perceived. She plans to advocate for mental health to help spread awareness in hopes of educating, if God were to allow also to help reform the mental-health laws, beginning in her state, California. Her mission is for the mentally ill to be properly treated in this country and in the whole world for that matter.

She resides in Southern California, and is married to the love of her life and has four beautiful children. She is a woman of faith. She owes all she is and has been given to God. And to Him, she gives the glory *always*. Amen.